a practical guide to
PUBLIC SPEAKING

by MAURICE FORLEY,
Executive Director of Toastmasters International

In the past forty years, Toastmasters International has launched more than half a million successful speakers. Each week throughout the world, over 80,000 members meet in more than 3,800 clubs to practice their skills. Now, based on his long experience as head of this famous organization, Maurice Forley provides the well-tested answers to the following questions:

- How to control tension
- How to select a subject
- How to organize and write speeches for all occasions
- How to deliver a talk effectively, with tips on voice control and stage presence
- How to handle a question period
- How to preside at a meeting
- How to find an audience, including special advice on working with service clubs

This is a truly up-to-date book on informal and formal speaking. It avoids the old cliches and takes into account the tastes and attitudes of a modern audience. Here also is an author who recognizes that today women may have as many opportunities to lecture as men and offers advice on dress, voice control, and approach, directed specifically at the ladies.

This is an indispensable guide for anyone, young or old, amateur or professional, who finds that he either must or wishes to speak in public. It is as useful to the clergyman who gives a weekly sermon as to the athlete suddenly confronted with an annual dinner. The busy executive forced to lecture on his special area will find it as helpful as the man with an unusual hobby who would like to reach fellow enthusiasts. Each chapter is filled with concrete examples. Excerpts from speeches range from a housewife's talk on baking to a congressman's political address.

A PRACTICAL GUIDE TO PUBLIC SPEAKING is the one book designed to help you from the first, possibly panicked moment, of accepting a speaking engagement through to your polished and confident delivery.

About the author:

MAURICE FORLEY lives in California, where in addition to heading Toastmasters International, he is a member of the board of directors of the Orange County Branch of Big Brothers and an Associate Professor of Speech at Orange State College.

a practical guide to
PUBLIC SPEAKING

Formerly titled:
PUBLIC SPEAKING WITHOUT PAIN

by MAURICE FORLEY

EXECUTIVE DIRECTOR

TOASTMASTERS INTERNATIONAL, INC.

Cover photograph — Tony Baron

Published by
Melvin Powers
WILSHIRE BOOK COMPANY
12015 Sherman Road
No. Hollywood, California 91605
Telephone: (213) 875-1711 / 983-1105

DEDICATION

I dedicate this book to the memory of my Father, to Dr. Ralph C. Smedley, and to the members of Toastmasters International.

COPYRIGHT © 1965 BY MAURICE FORLEY
Reprinted by arrangement with
David McKay Company, Inc.

All rights reserved, including the right to reproduce this book, or parts thereof, in any form, except for the inclusion of brief quotations in a review.

Toastmasters International encourages its members to think and speak for themselves. All the opinions in this book are not necessarily shared by Toastmasters International or all its members. However, the author is grateful to Toastmasters International, Inc., and to its President, Paris S. Jackson, for permission to quote from *The Toastmaster* magazine and other Toastmasters publications, including *The Amateur Chairman*, by Ralph C. Smedley.

Portions of the following are quoted with permission of the publishers: *Say It with Words*, by Charles W. Ferguson, Alfred A. Knopf, Inc.; *Mind in the Making*, by J. H. Robinson, Harper & Row; *Memories and Portraits*, by Robert Louis Stevenson, Charles Scribner's Sons; The Royal Bank of Canada *Monthly Letter*.

LIBRARY OF CONGRESS CATALOG CARD NUMBER: 65-11511
MANUFACTURED IN THE UNITED STATES OF AMERICA
ISBN 0-87980-121-2

Foreword

THIS book responds to a need that apparently has not been satisfied by the numerous texts and books of advice on public speaking now available.

The man or woman who is called upon occasionally to make a speech usually has neither the time nor the patience to wade through a lengthy college text designed to guide the student through a semester of intensive effort. On the other hand, most of the books intended for the average person (whoever that may be) supply more inspiration than information.

This book is practical rather than pretentious. It has been written to help the man or woman who wants to make a good impression with an effective talk and who does not have much time to prepare for the event.

This book attempts to answer the questions and doubts in the minds of the occasional speaker that are not covered in other books. This is a simple summary of the essentials of public speaking, based primarily on the successful experiences of thousands of men in Toastmasters clubs and on the suggestions of men and women in my public speaking classes. Within a short time almost all of them have developed the ability to deliver good speeches. They have found that successful public speaking without pain is neither as difficult nor as complex as they had anticipated.

I acknowledge gratefully my debt to all the Toastmasters and students who have made this book possible. There have also been many generous people whose contributions have helped to make it a reality.

Dr. Ralph C. Smedley, founder of Toastmasters International, and Dr. Seth A. Fessenden, Chairman of the Speech Department, California State College at Fullerton, have reviewed sections of the manuscript and have given me frequent counsel.

Successive international officers of Toastmasters have encouraged me and passed along to me their conclusions based on years of speechmaking experience.

For the material in Chapter 14, "How to Talk to a Service Club," I am indebted to John H. Vogt, Executive Administrator of Lions International; George R. Means, General Secretary, Rotary International; Bernard B. Burford, Secretary-Treasurer, Optimist International; and Richard C. Murray, Managing Director, Sertoma International.

Special acknowledgment is made to Fred DeArmond, Springfield, Missouri, author and a frequent contributor to *The Toastmaster* magazine. Mr. DeArmond assisted in preparing the outline, in writing drafts of a number of chapters, and with his critical reading of others. I am glad to say that by his efforts he has made important contributions to the substance and in some instances to the language of the book.

And then there is Mrs. Eleanor Rawson. I owe the existence of this book and much of any merit it may possess to Mrs. Rawson, Associate Editor of the David McKay Company. Her patient, tactful guidance, her steady encouragement, and her insistence on the best in every way have made this book far more rewarding to me than it can ever be to its readers.

I have also borrowed freely and without permission from Plutarch, Publilius Syrus, Thoreau, and Amiel. Without them and a host of other speakers and writers who have made public speaking one of the major factors in the development of our civilization, I should have had nothing to write about.

Table of Contents

	Introduction	xiii
1.	How to Use Fear	1
2.	How to Accept an Invitation	10
3.	How to Select a Subject	16
4.	How to Develop and Research Your Subject	27
5.	How to Extemporize, Memorize, or Read	34
6.	How to Organize Your Speech	48
7.	How to Write Your Speech	65
8.	How to Set the Stage	83
9.	How to Use Your Voice	95
10.	How to Influence Opinion	110
11.	How to Handle the Question Period	125
12.	How to Preside at a Meeting	134
13.	How to Find an Audience	149
14.	How to Talk to a Service Club	163
	Index	171

Introduction

You have opened this book because you are going to give a talk soon and you want some immediate, practical, specific help. Or perhaps you recognize that men and women of achievement are usually effective speakers, and you know you can help yourself by improving your speaking ability. This book has been written to help you make your next speech your best one and to help you become a better speaker with each succeeding speech.

As the Executive Director of Toastmasters International, I have enjoyed the unique privilege of learning from and working with eighty thousand men a year, all of whom are studying to speak more effectively. They range from Ph.D.'s to those who never finished grade school. They are at every economic level. Their jobs cover every legitimate method of making a living. Many are retired, and many have yet to earn their first pay check. They are in every one of the fifty United States, in each of the provinces of Canada, and in forty-two other countries. Some speak several languages; others have difficulty with one. They constitute the membership of the largest, oldest, most successful nonprofit, nonpartisan, nonsectarian educational organization in the world devoted to public speaking, or, more accurately, to self-fulfillment through self-expression.

In addition to working with Toastmasters, I have enjoyed the privilege of talking with officers of International Toastmistress Clubs about the special problems confronting women speakers, and I have borrowed heavily from their suggestions. ITC is entirely separate from Toastmasters, although it was organized by Toastmasters wives, and its principles and materials parallel those developed by the male organization.

In this book, I am passing along to you what we have taught and learned from people who have made more than a million speeches a year. For two generations, nearly three-quarters of a million men and women have applied these methods successfully. If they can do it, you can do it, too. They have proved that anyone who seriously wants to speak effectively to an audience has the potential ability to do so.

Good speakers are not born that way; the skill can be acquired. This book is written to prove that you, like most people, have the ability to become a public speaker. You will not find in these pages the secrets of great orators. In the first place, there are no secrets to the art. In the second place, it would not be honest or logical to imply that because Demosthenes spoke to the ocean waves with pebbles in his mouth and became one of the famed orators of history, you can become a great speaker by doing the same.

Therefore, instead of Demosthenes, I shall refer mostly to people who are just like you and have become excellent speakers through their application of the principles and methods described in these pages. Here let me mention only three of the many who took their first steps in public speaking through their association with Toastmasters clubs.

For example, Alex Smekta once froze to complete silence when he attempted to talk to a group of fellow workers. Today, having learned to talk easily, he owns his own business, is Mayor of Rochester, Minnesota, and has given speeches in many parts of the world as a representative of the United States Conference of Mayors.

Hazel Leona Lewis, whose full biography appears in *Who's Who of American Women,* attributes much of her success to her public speaking ability, which she developed as a Toastmistress. Presently the Postmaster of Stanton, California, Hazel Lewis is active in the League of Women Voters and is a leader among southern California women.

George J. Mucey, the son of a southern Illinois coal miner, aspired to be a professional baseball player. While playing for a St. Louis Cardinals farm team in a small Pennsylvania city, Mucey was injured and had to give up baseball. To qualify himself for a new occupation, he practiced public speaking in his club and wherever else he could. He became an insurance salesman and today owns one of the most successful life insurance agencies in the country. Mucey was recently given a testimonial dinner by the citizens of Washington, Pennsylvania, for his many services as one of its outstanding civic figures.

You are probably like these men in your desire to become a good public speaker. They did something about it. You are about to do the same.

Whether you read a paragraph, a chapter, or this entire book, you will learn something from the experience of others. There is no principle used by successful speakers that cannot be put into practice with noticeable results at once.

A word of warning: It is only fair to tell you what *not* to expect from this book. This is not a textbook, so you will find few rules or definitions and no classroom exercises. It is assumed that you are consulting this book because you do not have the time for an academic course in public speaking, nor do you seek credit for it. This is not an encyclopedia answering all questions on speaking. The subject matter has been selected to help you prepare and deliver your next speech—and many speeches thereafter.

In succeeding pages you will read the experience of many Toastmasters and Toastmistresses because the purpose of this book is to emphasize that the art of public speaking is not reserved for Winston Churchill, Franklin Delano Roosevelt, Margaret Mead, and other such prominent figures. Anybody can do it, including you—starting with your next speech.

CHAPTER 1

How to Use Fear

You will have an advantage at the outset if you free yourself from two false assumptions that prevent many aspirants from achieving the substantial rewards and satisfactions that come to the public speaker. The assumptions are:

1. That good speakers are born, not made; therefore it is useless to try unless you were endowed with a God-given talent.

2. That fear and nervousness are insurmountable for some persons. Therefore it is hopeless to attempt to conquer these apparent handicaps.

Let's consider each of these misconceptions.

Are Good Speakers Born and Not Made?

You don't really believe this, or you wouldn't be reading these pages. Everyone is born a baby, and babies can't speak. The "born speaker" myth is an excuse for not trying. The man or woman who accepts it is merely protecting his self-esteem from the risk of failure. The thousands who have successfully developed their latent abilities as public speakers, through Toastmasters and other organizations, have demonstrated beyond dispute that you can't fail to become a good speaker if you really want to and if you try.

A speaker is one who has the ability and the desire to talk to others for a purpose. When you were two or three years old and first said, "Daddy, I want a drink of water," you were making a speech. In fact, you've been making speeches ever since you could talk, although no one terrified you by pinning the label "speech" on your remarks and making you self-conscious about them.

You can become a speaker if you have these assets:

1. A voice.
2. Ordinary knowledge of language: that is, a working vocabulary and a reasonable acquaintance with grammar.
3. Something to say.
4. A desire to convey your thoughts to others.

You have been using these assets for years. You have been saying something to others, informally, dozens of times daily. Under these circumstances, you call it "conversation." Conversation is speech to the few. Public speaking is, basically, conversation adapted to a larger group.

Dr. Ralph C. Smedley, founder of Toastmasters International, offers this advice to beginners.

Remember that your audience is just a group of individuals. You usually can converse easily with one or two people. It is no harder when there are four or five individuals listening to you. An audience of a hundred people is made up of individuals, any one of whom you can talk with individually. Talk to the group as to one person.

Can You Overcome Fear?

Yes, there are three antidotes that will help you to minimize fear and make it work for you instead of against you: (1) recognize it; (2) analyze it; (3) utilize what you have learned.

1. *Recognize It*

You have no need to be afraid of fear when you recognize it as nature's way of protecting you and helping you. Accept it. Don't condemn yourself for your feelings. All men feel fear. Whether you are affected by distracting apprehension and tension when you think of yourself alone on the platform, facing hundreds of people, or whether you are touched by panic as you rise to speak, the *first thing to remember is that you are reacting normally.* You are not unique.

Athletes are jumpy before a crucial contest; musicians flutter internally before a concert; actors experience stage or mike fright. Experienced speakers never get rid of nervousness before speaking, nor do they want to. A seasoned performer once told me: "I used to have butterflies in my stomach whenever I faced an audience. Now that I know how to make them work for me, they fly in formation."

Knowing that you are subject to a normal and almost universal human reaction, you can dispel the strongest element contributing to your fear: *You can stop condemning yourself for being different.*

Psychologists tell us that fear is not the real problem. We feel guilty or cowardly or inadequate and therefore lack confidence in ourselves because we feel it to be unmanly or unflattering to feel fear.

Think about that: It is not fear, but your feeling about your fear, that upsets you. Franklin Roosevelt's paraphrase of the words of Henry Thoreau sums it up: "We have nothing to fear but fear itself." Once you recognize this and accept it, you are well along the road to self-mastery.

Fear is nature's way of helping you to protect yourself and to prepare yourself to confront real or fancied dangers. When you face a new or different situation in which you want to do well, or when many are watching you and failure or mistakes may be humiliating, nature does something wonderful that helps you to excel yourself, if you accept the help instead of being upset by it. Nature increases the adrenalin in your blood stream; it quickens your pulse and your reactions, raises your blood pressure, and makes you more alert, equipping you for the extra effort you need to do your best. If you didn't feel nervous, you would not do as well. Recognize fear as a friend. Accept it and use it.

2. *Analyze Your Fear*

Your second step in mastering fear is quick and painless. Analyze your kind of fear. I've said fear is a device for self-protection. What are you protecting? You are concerned about your ego, your self-esteem. In public speaking there are only three threats to your self-esteem. These barriers to the achievement of confidence and success take the following forms.

(*a*) You may be afraid of yourself—afraid of performing badly or not satisfying your ego.

(*b*) You may be afraid of your audience—afraid *they* may laugh at or dislike you.

(*c*) You may be afraid of your material—afraid you have nothing worth while to say or are not well prepared.

Fear of yourself (*a*) and fear of your audience (*b*) are very closely related. It is conceivable that you might satisfy yourself while failing to please your audience, but in most instances you will be speaking for the purpose of winning audience approval. Therefore, if you succeed with them, you are really succeeding with yourself. Admit this.

However, in aiming to please your audience you must never belie your real convictions or suppress your conscience. There are occasions when you will face an audience hostile to your honestly expressed thoughts. This calls for a positive display of courage. But you need not be afraid to disagree. Many of the best speakers have done so and have walked off the platform proudly and triumphantly. Sincere convictions arm a speaker and give power to his utterances.

3. *Utilize What You Have Learned*

You have recognized your fear and accepted it as nature's secret weapon to help you succeed. You have analyzed it and found that you are not really afraid of fear but afraid of yourself, your audience, or your material. Now the time has come to *utilize* your knowledge. Here's how you can do so.

(*a*) *Conceal your negative feelings from others.* If you reflect a lack of confidence, a feeling of awkwardness or insecurity, it will show. Therefore, the first thing you must do is learn to conceal your negative feelings; you gain nothing by letting the audience realize that you are frightened. Whether you are nervous a week in advance of your speaking date or as you mount the stage, don't talk about it. This will only make you feel worse. A surprising thing will happen if you act highly self-confident: some of your act will rub off on you. You will begin to *feel* the way you appear to be. Remember the case of the frightened boy walking past the cemetery on a dark night? As long as he walked casually and whistled gaily he was fine. When he decided to walk faster, he could not resist the temptation to run; and when he ran, stark terror took over. Don't take that first fast step. Don't give in. Don't show fear, and don't talk about it.

(*b*) *Appraise your situation realistically.* Recall the reasons why *you* were invited to speak. *You* were selected —not any one of dozens of other people or any of those in your audience. Whoever extended the invitation had confidence in you, or you would not have been selected. You are capable of speaking well, and you know your subject. You know more about it than your audience does.

Ethel Merman has said that she does not suffer in anticipation of an audience or in front of it because of fear of inability to perform well. She assures herself that if the audience could perform better, they would be on the stage. She knows her audience believes she will perform better than they can; that's one reason they admire her and come to see and hear her. This is an appropriate amount of conceit that you and all speakers are entitled to, and it is nothing more than a proper respect for yourself.

Your appraisal of the situation reveals that you are prepared to do well and that you have the advantage over your audience. Once you believe this, your confident conduct and attitude will communicate itself to your listeners and help them to accept you and your message.

(c) *Appraise your audience realistically.* Remember that they want you to do well. Audiences suffer with the speaker who is having a struggle, and they do not enjoy suffering. They would much rather respond to you pleasantly and have a good time. So think about your audience instead of yourself. Win their interest, and you will find it difficult to fear those who have only friendly feelings toward you.

Dr. Robert T. Oliver, author of *The Psychology of Persuasive Speech*, gave this advice about speakers and their audiences in the April, 1958, issue of *The Toastmaster* magazine.

When a man has a message to deliver to his fellows, it is the message that counts, more than its packaging. Instead of being "separated" from his listeners, every effort should be made to make them feel he is one of them, in spirit, in purpose and in manner. A real leader is, first, genuinely "one of the group," and secondly, superior to the group—in knowledge, in courage, in insight, in skill. But always and forever, we influence our fellows only as we first make it clear we are with them—and are interested in *them*, not in a display of ourselves.

Another way of putting this thought is: Concentrate on expressing your ideas, not on impressing the listeners with your wisdom and cleverness. Do the first well, and the second will follow.

(*d*) *Appraise your material realistically.* Fear of your speech material is the easiest form of fear to overcome because you possess the complete remedy for it: knowledge and preparation. Dr. R. C. Smedley offers this comment:

The antidote to fear is knowledge. If the novice knows that he knows his subject, he has taken the first step in the conquest of fear. Knowledge inspires self-confidence, and knowledge plus confidence will overcome fear. The unprepared speaker has a right to be scared. His own neglect imposes the fear based on ignorance.

Knowledge and preparation allay fear, but by themselves they do not necessarily guarantee the delivery of an effective speech. In later chapters we shall discuss the kind of preparation needed and how to acquire and utilize knowledge.

At this point, as you appraise your own attitude and aptitudes and start work on that speech you will make next Thursday, you have made a good beginning because you know you need not be afraid—of yourself, your audience, or your material. Next Thursday you are going to find that you *can* do it. With the completion of each successive talk you will not only say, "I *can* do it!" with growing conviction and confidence; you will say, "I *can* do it because I *have* done it."

Summary

Effective public speakers are made, not born. You can become an effective public speaker if you know how to master your fear. To master your fear and make it work for you, you must do three things.

1. Recognize it as nature's way of helping you.
2. Analyze it and pinpoint the form affecting you: (a) fear of disappointing yourself; (b) fear of disappointing your audience; (c) fear of your material.
3. Utilize your knowledge.

There are four ways to use your knowledge of fear in your favor.

1. *Conceal your negative feelings from others.* If you show your lack of confidence in yourself, your audience will lack confidence in you. If you act self-confident, you will feel more self-confident and speak with confidence. "As a man speaks, so is he."

2. *Appraise your situation realistically.* You were selected to speak; you know your subject; your audience is for you. All the advantages rest with you. You will share an enjoyable experience with your audience.

3. *Appraise your audience realistically.* They do not know as much as you know about your subject; they want to hear from you and want you to succeed for their sake.

4. *Appraise your material realistically.* You know your subject; you have prepared yourself and your material; therefore, you will satisfy your audience and yourself.

CHAPTER 2

How to Accept an Invitation

MANY of those entrusted with the assignment don't truly know how to invite a speaker. Often, they have never been on the receiving end of an invitation and are unable to put themselves in the speaker's position. Therefore, they do not provide him with the information he must have if he is to plan and deliver a talk suitable to the occasion and the audience.

You will probably have to help the person who invites you to speak. Don't hesitate to tell him you need certain information to enable you to do a good job. You will avoid wasted effort and awkward situations and increase the probability of your effectiveness if you are fully informed on these subjects: (1) the arrangements; (2) the occasion; (3) the audience; (4) what is expected of you.

The Arrangements

Be sure you are clear on how and when you are to meet your audience and have a written reminder on the pertinent details.

1. Learn the date and hour.
2. Identify and locate the meeting place. Obtain more specific information than just "Congregational Church on North Oak Street." There may be two churches on North Oak. If your audience is to be in Room C, Annex, write that down, too, and get directions on how to reach the Annex.
3. Who will meet you? It may not be the same person who extended the invitation.
4. Who will introduce you? You should know something about the man or woman so that you can make appropriate acknowledgment of the introduction if you desire.
5. Is the room equipped with lectern, public address system, microphone, blackboard? Will a meal be served?

When a general is preparing for a military engagement he studies the terrain; when an experienced traveler is planning an automobile trip he studies road conditions. You need to know the conditions you will meet so that you can adapt your speech and its delivery. We shall discuss these factors affecting your speech in more detail later in the book.

The Occasion

1. Will the affair mark an anniversary or have any special purpose? Your talk must be in good taste and appro-

priate to the occasion. If you are to speak at a dinner honoring the City School Superintendent on his retirement, you will not wish to give a talk on "What's Wrong with Our Schools Today?"

2. Is the affair one that requires formal dress? If you are a woman, you will probably wish to find out the exact degree of formality.

3. What about the rest of the program on which you will appear? Will you be the only speaker? Program committees often overload their time. If you find yourself last on a lengthy list of speakers or events, the audience may be tired or bored. You may need to shorten your speech and spice it with stories and human interest in order to hold your audience.

The Audience

Get some facts about the composition of the audience as to sex, age, vocation, special interests. Recently a Santa Ana women's club asked me to invite a Toastmaster to talk on their luncheon program "on any interesting subject." I referred the invitation to a member visiting us from Arizona. I had heard him speak and knew he was good. "What shall I talk about?" he asked. Since I knew that most of the ladies were from Iowa and other midwestern areas, I suggested that he tell them about life on his large ranch in the desert.

A short time after the meeting I met one of the club members and asked her about the speech. "It was horrible!" she said. "All he talked about was the rattlesnake problem on his ranch. And his description of how to kill a rattlesnake was so vivid, few of us could eat our lunch!"

A direct inquiry would have helped.

What Is Expected of You

1. What subject might be appropriate, and how should you treat it? Sheldon Hayden, head of the Department of Speech, Santa Monica Junior College, and a former President of Toastmasters International, says:

Big business has discovered the importance of launching a market investigation to determine the wants of the consumer in a product before it is offered for sale. In public speech it is vital to determine the interests of an audience in choosing a subject. Consideration of their interests, problems, and aspirations will give the key to many subjects suitable for the audience, and will save you the embarrassment of presenting some theme on which the crowd is cold. The selection of a theme that will interest the audience determines about 50 per cent of the success of a speech. The other 50 per cent is made up of your personality and the ideas which you, as a speaker, have to present.

I know a doctor who is proud of his ability as a humorous speaker. He was invited to give a talk on the subject of baldness. It was a very funny talk. This time it fell flat. His audience was a Senior Citizens Club, most of whose members were bald. Beware, therefore, of accepting any subject that is proposed to you. Always test its fitness yourself.

More than likely, the choice of a topic will be left to you. Find out whether your host wishes you to entertain, inspire, inform, or move the audience to action. Accurate information as to what is wanted will help you choose a subject and decide how to deal with it.

Give your material a catchy title. When the State Dental Hygienists Society invited me to tell their convention how to make an informal talk, my title was "How to Avoid Foot-in-Mouth Disease." I was told that this was useful for publicity purposes and helped draw a large audience.

2. "Why was I asked to speak?" If you get little help from your host regarding the composition and interests of your audience, you should ask this question of yourself. If your hobby is speleology and you enjoy a local reputation for your activities in this field, it is reasonable to suppose the program committee assumed you would talk about caves, and the audience expects this of you. If, instead, you give a talk about astronomy based on your study of an article in the encyclopedia, you may disappoint a lot of people.

3. How much time is allotted to your talk? If you are not told, be sure to find out; then adhere to it. No matter how interesting your talk may be, if you dwell on your subject much beyond the time allowance, you upset the schedule of the planning committee. You increase the risk of wearing out your welcome and losing the effectiveness of your speech by going beyond an appropriate ending. In any event, you will have been discourteous and inconsiderate if your talk is longer than expected.

If no time limit has been given you, bear in mind the formula Professor John Chester Adams, adviser to the Yale University Debate Team, once gave me: "If, as far as you've gone, it's been a good speech, it's time to stop. If, as far as you've gone, it's been a disappointing speech, it's a hell of a good time to stop."

Self-Helps

Finally, there are several things you can do to increase the probability of a successful speaking engagement by *writing a letter* covering the following points.

1. Confirm the details of the meeting, including the time, place, length of speech, and subject. If there has been any misunderstanding, your letter will lead to its correction.
2. After stating your title, amplify its theme in a couple of sentences.
3. Supply a few facts that can be used in introducing you.
4. Give some of your background that may be helpful in publicizing your appearance.

Summary

1. When you receive an invitation to speak, obtain information about the arrangements, the occasion, the audience, and the kind of talk you are expected to present.
2. After you have selected an appropriate subject, give your talk an appealing title.
3. Write a letter confirming your acceptance. State your understanding as to the time and place of the meeting. Give your speech title and a few facts about yourself that may be useful in publicizing your talk and that may help the chairman in introducing you.

CHAPTER 3

How to Select a Subject

You have accepted the obligation to interest your audience by agreeing to give a talk. Obviously, without a subject you would have nothing to say. Therefore, your work begins with finding answers to two vital questions.
1. What shall I talk about?
2. How can I make my subject interesting?

What Shall I Talk About?

This cardinal principle is clear: If *you* are not interested in a subject, you cannot make it interesting to your audience. Your indifference will show. Therefore, you must begin your search by considering what subjects interest you. I am surprised repeatedly by the number of men and women who want to become good public speakers but have no lively interest in the world around them and consequently have no ideas to share. If you have no enthusiasms, no reactions or thoughts about the simple or complex marvels among which you live—in short, if you have nothing to say and no urge to communicate with others—don't waste your time or that of your audience. Don't make a speech.

However, your budding interest in public speaking can open the door to a fascinating new universe, for an attitude of observation and appreciation can be cultivated. You have senses, a brain, and a heart; you have the basic equipment for developing the seeing eye, the hearing ear, the inquiring mind, and the human affection needed to get the most out of living and to give something to others.

Ask questions. Why do you read this page from left to right? Was this always the case? Are there other languages that read from right to left or from top to bottom? How long is a red traffic signal? Why that length? Why is the green signal above the red light—or is it? What do color-blind drivers do about traffic signals?

Constantly ask *who, what, where, how,* and, most productive of all, *why* in the manner of newspaper reporters, and you'll uncover a wealth of intriguing ideas and material. Once you have determined your own interests, choose the topic for your speech from among them.

Four Steps in Developing Ideas

To come down to cases, here are four steps for prying open your new world of ideas and mining its treasure of speaking topics.

1. *Observe* the world around you.

2. *Learn* about what you see. Ask questions: What does it mean? Why is it like this? How did it come to be? Where will it lead?

3. *Judge* what you observe and learn. Armed with facts of life and knowledge about them, you are ready to form an opinion. Do you like what you have found? Does it seem good or bad?

4. *Act* on your judgment of the facts and your understanding of them. What can be done about them? How can you encourage others to do it?

I am sure that you recognize in this summary of the formula just another way of defining the essentials of a good speech: Have something to say and a desire to communicate—for a purpose. If you follow the formula, you will supply yourself with many subjects. More than that, you will have provided for yourself a purpose and a program.

Build a Subject File

You do not now remember all the subjects that aroused your interest during the past month. Undoubtedly there were quite a few. Don't lose good subjects through your own negligence. Start a file. Add to it from newspapers and magazines, references to books as you read them, and notes drawn from radio, television, and other speakers. Keep a diary in which you record bits of conversation, ideas, and your introspections. Henri Frédéric Amiel, one of the great journal writers, followed this practice throughout his life because of his belief that a man's conversation with himself is a gradual process of clarifying his own thoughts.

Now: Which Subject for Me?

At this point, your question is no longer "What shall I talk about?" but "Of all the subjects that interest me, which shall I select?"

1. *Select a topic that you have special qualifications to handle.* Your interest may flame high over Cuba, the civil rights of a minority group, or Spinoza's philosophy, but do you have special information or experience that others probably do not have? William Jennings Bryan said that the prerequisite of eloquence is for the speaker to have great enthusiasm about worth-while subjects on which he is thoroughly informed. Thoroughness based on knowledge or experience is an important element. Talk about what you know.

2. *Be yourself.* In choosing your subject, be sure that it is "in character" for you, and then be yourself in dealing with it. Despite his keen sense of humor and interest in the foibles of his fellow men, Albert Einstein never tried to sound like Bob Hope. It wouldn't have "come out right." Will Rogers was interested in politics and qualified to talk on the subject. However, he never tried to sound like Herbert Hoover. He just said that his only knowledge came from reading the papers, and then he proceeded to comment on the news in his own style.

Mark Twain and Bret Harte came from similar background. Both had been journalists in the Far West and had written with humor about that setting. After becoming successful as writers, each went east and took to the lecture platform. Mark Twain talked like himself and became a huge success as a speaker. Harte ignored the direct, homespun style that brought him fame and tried to be somebody other than himself in talking about subjects he knew. He stepped out of character and failed as a speaker.

3. *What do you know best?*

(*a*) Talk about your job. You know your subject; you are qualified to talk about it. With the exercise of a little imagination and sensitivity to other people, you can select some aspect of your work that will intrigue your audience. If you are a lawyer, talk about how a client looks to his lawyer or what a lawyer needs to know if he is to help his client. If you are a dentist, discuss what you like—or dislike—about patients. If you are a city employee, describe how the public looks from your side of the desk and how citizens can best get results in dealing with you. If you are a veterinary, tell what you have learned about people from treating their pets.

In short, give your audience something more than a job description. They may be mildly interested in what you do, but they will probably have great interest in what they do, as you see them in your job.

(*b*) Talk about your hobby—but be careful of this one. Your audience knows you enjoy it, or it wouldn't be your hobby. Before you tell your listeners much about it, you must arouse their interest and curiosity. You must give them a reason why your hobby should be attractive to them: some unique or fascinating facts, some relation between your collection of campaign buttons and national history, some evidence of the rewards and satisfaction your hobby may hold for them, not you.

(*c*) Talk about your travels. If you have visited Berlin recently, you have a ready-made subject for an engrossing travel talk, providing you have something to say that has not already been said by TV commentators and others. Mayor Alex Smekta of Rochester, Minnesota, made the trip with a group of American mayors. He took along his notebook and camera, and in Berlin he talked with every resident he was able to buttonhole. On his return to the United States, Mayor Smetka did not discourse on the political implications of the Berlin Wall: he talked about the feelings of people whose lives were affected by it. Within six months of his first address, he received more than a hundred invitations to speak to other groups. The reason for his popularity was that he had an interesting approach to an interesting subject.

However, if you have not visited Berlin, gone backstage at the Folies Bergères, or traveled the sewers of Paris, you may still have material for a good travel talk. Henry Thoreau said he had traveled widely in Concord. I have a friend in New York City who takes walks in a different section of the city every Sunday. His ever-changing talk entitled "The Sidewalks of New York" reflects conditions, events, and observations that have held the interest of clubs and luncheon groups in several states. He has developed an enjoyable and profitable side-line activity based on his leisure-time interest. Remember, your audience will be more engaged by what you learned in London from your Cockney cab driver than in your confirmation of the dimensions of Westminster Abbey.

(*d*) Talk about ideas and issues—but only if you have reasonable grounds for believing that you can give your listeners new insight, new knowledge, new ideas, or more penetrating thought and analysis than they have within themselves. Otherwise, you are just one more person with an opinion. When there is no special reason for the audience to listen to you, you have lost one of your chief reasons for making a speech—or being heard.

4. *Some special tips for women.*

Many women have told me, "I'm only a housewife! I don't have a job and I have never traveled. What can I talk about that others would want to hear?"

Instead of being handicapped, housewives have an advantage in selecting subjects because they have so much more in common with their audience! The only additional ingredient you need, if you are a housewife, is imagination and perhaps a sense of humor or an appreciation of new approaches to everyday subjects. I suspect that most married women will listen attentively to "How to Handle Husbands," or more specifically, "How to Handle a Hostile Husband." Speeches on home management, how to get along with the neighbors, how to shop, how to secure neighborhood improvements, how to help children meet their problems, or even "What I Do with My 'Woman's Rights'" are of interest to other women. And almost any subject that lends itself to fresh scrutiny from the feminine viewpoint will interest men. "A Woman Looks At..." is an arresting title that will appeal to most men just because of their basic interest in women and their general lack of knowledge about the way some women reason.

How Can I Make My Subject Interesting?

Second only to selecting a topic that appeals to you is the technique of making it appeal to your audience.

Consider Your Subject from the Viewpoint of Your Listeners

While you may not know enough about your audience to determine what subjects they will like, you may be sure that any topic you decide upon will hold greater interest for them if you treat it from their viewpoint. You will recall that in discussing your job as a subject for a talk, I suggested that you orient your treatment to recognize the *other person's* outlook on your job rather than your own. In discussing your hobby, I suggested that you consider why your hobby might appeal to others rather than why it is a favorite of yours.

In one of my speech classes, a housewife who loved to bake gave a speech on "How to Bake Yeast Rolls." The subject interested her, but not her audience, as she described it. A week later she gave essentially the same talk, but her title reflected a different point of view: "How You, Too, Can Make Yeast Rolls." She thought and then talked about her subject from the viewpoint of her audience rather than herself, and this alone made a decided difference. She has given the revised speech before a number of women's clubs and is now something of a local authority on her hobby.

Learn to Vary Your Approach

Do you wish your audience to form their own opinions on a subject, or are you hoping to sway them to share your opinion? In the first case, you will need only to present your material in an interesting manner. In the second case, you will probably wish to begin by arousing their emotions, continue by appealing to their intellects, and conclude by explaining the best ways in which they can channel their reactions constructively. The specific techniques you use to persuade your audience will depend on whom you are addressing and the nature of your subject (see Chapter 10).

Don't Bite Off More than You Can Chew

Next to selecting a subject that he knows only superficially, the most common mistake of an inexperienced speaker is to choose too broad a subject or one that cannot be covered effectively in the allotted time. The scientist who spoke to the luncheon club on "The Theory and History of Organic Evolution" bit off more than he (or his audience) could handle in the twenty-five minutes allotted for his talk. So did the army corporal who tried to cover in ten minutes "The Nomenclature, Function, and Employment of Infantry Weapons."

Fred DeArmond cites this hypothetical case in *A Guide to Personal Success in Management*. A traveler, returning from a jaunt around the world, was asked by a program chairman to talk on "The Present Political Situation Around the World." The speaker realized that this took in too much territory and modified his subject to "The Westward March of the Communist Ideology." A little reflection convinced him that here, again, was too large an undertaking. For a thirty-minute speech he decided to make it "Communism's Appeal in South America and Asia." When he got down to the business of writing his speech, he decided that a more manageable subject would be "How Communists Sell Their Program in Brazil."

Be sure to decide carefully whether the subject you select can be handled in the time assigned to you.

Summary

To capture the interest of your audience, you must have an interesting subject; to hold your audience, you must say something interesting about the subject.

Find Plenty of Subjects

1. Select a subject in which you are interested, but do not assume that your audience will react to it just because you do.
2. If you do not have a subject, develop a taste for many subjects by asking *who, what, where, how,* and *why* as you go about your daily life.
3. When a subject appeals to you, observe and learn all you can about it, form an opinion, and then decide what you want to do about your conclusions.
4. Build a card file of subjects; it is good to have more than you can possibly use.

Choose One for Yourself—and Your Audience

1. Select a subject that you are uniquely qualified to discuss.
2. Be yourself in talking about it. This means more than "being natural"; it means you should stay in character. (A good actor seems natural in other characters; as public speakers, we aim to be natural as ourselves.)
3. If you talk about your job, hobby, or travels, look for angles that will interest your audience rather than those that appeal to you.

4. Vary your approach, depending on whether you wish your audience to form their own opinions on a subject or whether you are hoping to sway them to share your opinion.

5. Select a subject you can cover effectively in the time allotted.

CHAPTER 4

How to Develop and Research Your Subject

HAVING selected your subject, the next step in preparing your speech is to develop something to say about it. Undoubtedly you had some ideas that helped persuade you to select your subject, but the difference between a few ideas and an effective speech replete with good material is the difference between success and failure. When you accepted the responsibility of giving a speech, you gave an implied promise that you would have something to say that would deserve the attention of your audience.

How to Develop Your Material

There are three ways to help yourself build upon your topic. They all require effort and preparation. I do not know of any good public speaker who has achieved recognition without working at it.

Preparation and effort are two essential ingredients that *only you can supply*. Books such as this can offer only guidance and the lessons others have learned from experience. As my father used to say, "A minister can't have religion for his congregation." We can help you give direction to your effort, and we can help make your preparation painless, but *only you* can make yourself an effective speaker.

Take an Inventory

Before preparing to write a speech, sit down and take an inventory of what you already know, the points you think you want to make, and a list of possible sources of information you may need. It may be a sorry, unimpressive string of seemingly unrelated topics and bare facts having nothing in common but their pertinence to your subject. Never mind; it's a start, and getting started is one of the hardest steps in preparing a speech. This chore will do much for you.

1. It will start a flow of ideas. Ideas somehow have a way of multiplying themselves. You may be surprised at the number of thoughts that will be stimulated by the exercise of writing your inventory.

2. It will indicate the areas in which you need more information and bring to mind questions you are presently unable to answer. In other words, the inventory will help you to determine specifically the research you need to undertake when you go to the library.

3. Your list, kept in a notebook, will help you live with your subject and make you sensitive to items in the daily

paper, or lines from an unrelated book, that you can apply. You will induce a mood that causes you to think about your subject as you drive home from work or while you are awaiting your turn in the barber's chair or the beauty parlor. You'll be surprised at the unexpected dividends your mind will yield if you keep such an inventory in an ever-present pocket notebook. This inventory will also prepare you to make the most of the methods for preparing speech material.

Reach Out

If you are willing to make the effort, here are three methods of preparing the substance of any speech.

1. *Talk to a wide range of people about your topic.* If the subject is taxation, talk with the assessor as well as with taxpayers. If traffic safety is your subject, talk to a highway patrolman, an ambulance driver, a tow-car driver, and survivors of accidents. You will obtain vivid, first-person information and unexpected human-interest material that will liven your talk, and you will sound much more persuasive as you speak with firsthand authority.

You will have taken an important step toward becoming a speech craftsman because you will be practicing a principle known to writers and speakers as *individualizing with specific detail*. Specific, concrete allusions are much more effective than generalizations.

Even if your subject is an abstraction, talk with others about it. You will obtain fresh viewpoints, new ideas, and frequently a well-turned phrase or a helpful quotation from an authoritative source. You will also have an opportunity to test reactions to your ideas—a boon to any speaker.

2. *Use experiences from daily life.* Women, and especially housewives equipped with curiosity, have opportunities to develop ideas into rewarding speeches. Recently I attended a Toastmistress Club meeting where the "Best Speech of the Evening" award went to a mother of three children, whose talk was entitled "How to Eat Your Way Around the World Without Leaving Home."

To interest her children in geography, the speaker had taken them to the Chinese section of the city. The children enjoyed their luncheon at a Chinese restaurant, so their mother took them to a Chinese grocery next door. She made some purchases and experimented at home with a few Chinese recipes, which were well received. From this experience, it was a direct and simple step to Japanese, Mexican, Indian, Italian, and French cooking. The children read library books to learn about the children of other countries who ate the intriguing dishes that appeared on the family dinner table. The home-bound travelers gained weight from the combined diet of foreign fare and library books, and their school grades also benefited.

Curiosity about a detergent used for washing dishes led another speaker to the growing threat to city drinking water caused by such products. A can of tomatoes led to a talk on the history of canned goods and their unique place in American life.

Any man or woman who will pause a few times a day to ask "Why?" or "How come?" will be rewarded with ideas that lead to the library and thence to the lectern with a rewarding speech about the tools of daily life that most of us take for granted.

3. *Go to the books.* Educate yourself with the ideas of others, with reports of their experience, with statistics, if

appropriate. Go to the library. One of the best speeches I have ever heard was given by a housewife in my public speaking class. The title of her talk was "How to Kill Your Children." Her subject was the common examples of carelessness around the house that can, and sometimes do, cause the death of children.

The subject occurred to the speaker when she discovered that her three-year-old son had climbed onto the kitchen table and had eaten enough laxative pills to make him very sick. The week before, she had persuaded him to take one of the pills by telling him it was candy. The guilt-stricken mother wondered how many casualties occurred among children, from comparable household situations, in which parents were unintentionally responsible. Her inquiry led her from the kitchen table to the local library. She found statistics and examples, ranging from suffocation fatalities caused by plastic clothes bags and by discarded deep-freeze units that should have been hauled away, to poisoning from eating cleaning powder that is too often kept under the kitchen sink.

Tips on Using a Library

If your research is extended, you'll need to compile a bibliography to work from. In a public library the first source is the card index of books, classified three ways: by title, subject, and author. A second launching pad is the *Readers' Guide*, in which the principal articles in all the leading magazines are indexed—an excellent source for general material. Third is the *Industrial Arts Index* of business and technical journals, if you are heading into economic and scientific fields. Fourth, use the *New York*

Times Index. The *Times* is the only newspaper in the country that is indexed for general library use.

These are the major reference sources. The librarian will tell you about other specialized reference works for biography, education, poetry, essays, etc. Do not overlook the almanacs, or books of facts, and the encyclopedias. Anyone who does much speaking should have these primary tools, plus a good dictionary and a thesaurus or word finder, in his own home or office library.

A Note on Note Taking

There are various ways of recording information to be used in a speech. Some researchers note their data on cards, preferably 4 by 6 inches. Others prefer the more compact loose-leaf book. Use alphabetical dividers in such a book and separate sheets for each memo, which should be placed in the appropriate alphabetical section.

Make your notes in sufficient detail so that you won't have to puzzle over their meaning later. Use quotation marks only for material that is directly quoted. If you add your own comments for adaptation, distinguish them from the author's words or your abstract of them by enclosing in parentheses.

Along with your search for needed facts, keep on the lookout for short "sparklers," pertinent anecdotes, and current news pegs that will help to point up and spice your speech.

In material taken from books, append title, author, publisher, year of publication, and page. Similarly identify magazines, publication issue, and author. Getting these facts down at the time may save you labor later if you go back to confirm something.

Above all, if you plan to quote someone's actual words, be sure to copy them *exactly*, to the last comma and period, while the original is before you. Misquoting is not only poor scholarship and bad manners; it is potentially perilous.

Summary

The difference between a few ideas and a well-developed speech is the difference between success and failure. To develop your material:

1. Take an inventory of what you know about your subject and what you will have to fill in. This stimulates the flow of ideas and analogies.

2. Talk to a wide range of people with firsthand information.

3. Use experiences from daily life.

4. Go to books and other printed matter.

(*a*) Learn your way around a library.

(*b*) Store your research material through systematic note taking.

CHAPTER 5

How to Extemporize, Memorize, or Read

THE way you deliver a speech can determine its success. What method is the best for you? The only way to find out is to test yourself by trying out the different methods available to you. An important part of the answer is finding out how you can most quickly prompt yourself mentally when you are speaking.

We can divide all speeches into three classes, as far as preparation and delivery go: (1) impromptu; (2) extemporaneous; (3) formal.

The Impromptu Speech

This is the speech delivered on the spur of the moment, without specific preparation for the occasion. Usually it is quite short. You are present at a meeting; you're not on the program; but the chairman invites you to make a few remarks or asks for your view of an issue under consideration. Perhaps you are not very interested and really have nothing particular to say. But to say so would be rude, and you would miss an occasion for developing yourself as a speaker.

Since you want experience speaking you should take advantage of all opportunities to acquire ease. If you have any notion that you may be called on, formulate in advance some brief point that you can make if the chance comes up. Your comments should seem spontaneous and be made without referring to notes.

Another way to get experience in impromptu speaking is to go to meetings where you know subjects will come up on which you have strong convictions and can add pertinent information. Perhaps some glaring fallacy is voiced; then, in due course, ask for permission to refute it. Or if a discussion period will follow a speech, wait and pin down the speaker with a question that will expose his error. Honest emotion can provide inspiration for articulate and effective impromptu talks.

If you speak impromptu, do it briefly. Have something on tap in your mind, remembering Mark Twain's quip that it took him about three weeks to prepare a good impromptu speech. Drive home one sharp point; then sit down. Don't rely on filling a regular speaking engagement impromptu.

The Extempore Speech

When we refer to the extemporaneous speech, we usually mean one that is spoken from notes and not written out. Daniel Webster's famous reply to Hayne was delivered in the Senate from notes that he had jotted down on several sheets of paper. In answer to a question about his speech, he said that his whole life had been a preparation for that effort. It is generally regarded as the masterpiece of the most eloquent American.

While words and form can be extemporized, they cannot mask a lack of thought. Webster's views had been clearly formulated. He had only to clothe them in appropriate language, which came readily to his fluent mind since he had given much study to the Constitution as an unbreakable compact among the states.

H. V. Kaltenborn has usually extemporized in his radio and TV talks and also his platform appearances. For a one-hour lecture he has often used topic cards with a few factual notes. Sometimes he has written out his final sentence in advance, but he confesses that he usually forgets to use it. Actually, Mr. Kaltenborn says his best extemporaneous speeches were based on material he was familiar with, which had been distilled and carefully organized in his mind beforehand. There is no real substitute for preparation.

No one understood and applied this better than Winston Churchill, who always seemed to speak on the spur of the moment, without effort. When he was in North America on one of his wartime visits, he agreed to make a network radio broadcast before returning home. A date was set two weeks ahead. During that time (according to his war memoirs) the speech engagement "hung over me like a vulture in the sky." It would seem that Churchill could have spoken on the progress of the war at a moment's notice and at any length. But he took all his speaking engagements seriously and prepared for them meticulously.

Notes Are Reminders

If you speak from notes, you need to be free to think about *what* you are saying while you are saying it. You must know your material. Your notes should serve only as reminders of the points you want to make and of their order. To speak effectively from notes, cultivate word facility in the ways suggested in Chapter 7. If you are a beginner, you will have to develop this faculty as you progress. You can do it only through practice, by using every available opportunity to speak in public and by persistent rehearsing. Don't assume the sublime assurance of the young man who, when asked if he could play the piano, replied, "I don't know; I've never tried."

One of the difficulties you have to beat in extemporaneous speaking is a tendency to hash over too frequently one point or idea from your notes. Don't practice in front of your audience. Do that at home first. Some may be able to memorize their notes under five or six topical heads so that they don't need to refer to them. Even so, it's safer to have the notes at hand.

How to Use Notes

You alone can determine whether to use notes. If you use them, do not act ashamed of them. Don't be furtive. Use 3 by 5 inch cards and hold them comfortably in one hand, bringing the notes up within reading range only when you want to refer to them. Or place them on the lectern and look at them only when you need to do so. Don't fiddle with them.

Toastmaster Charles Michaels, Jr., a construction management engineer for the United States government, had this to say in the January, 1962, *Toastmaster* magazine:

Notes can be compared, as they often are, to crutches. If a man breaks his leg and relies constantly on crutches, he is in trouble. If he throws his crutches away before his leg is healed, he's in trouble. But wise is the man who uses his crutches properly, exercises and strengthens his leg and then when he knows and has demonstrated his readiness, uses them no longer. So it is with notes. I still take notes with me to the lectern. I never use them, but I take them anyway. I believe in them as insurance.

Possibly a Written Draft

Some extemporizers prefer to write a speech out, to get it set in their minds in logical order without actually memorizing it. If you do this, many words, phrases, and sentences in your full manuscript will pop into mind more or less unconsciously when you get up to speak and will help you to dress your remarks in vigorous language. This method comes very close to that of the formal speech.

The Formal Speech

"Formal," in this connection, has no reference to black tie or white, but to the speech that is written out. When you have the time, and when the occasion is important to you, this procedure is recommended.

After you outline and write your speech, in full or in part, there are three ways of delivering it.

1. Memorize the written speech and deliver it word for word.

2. Read the speech from a manuscript.

3. Deliver it from the outline or abbreviated notes based on the outline.

Memorizing

Experts agree that memorizing is not the right course. It is too slow and laborious. A thirty-minute speech will run to more than four thousand words, or about thirteen pages of double-spaced typescript. But even a shorter speech should not be memorized. A lapse in your memory results in an embarrassing pause. In groping for a lost word or phrase, you start floundering, your thought lost in the search for words. Don't tax your memory this way. Concentrate on delivering ideas, not on remembering details.

To Read or Not to Read

The prejudice against reading a speech is gradually dying, as more and more able speakers indulge in the practice. There are many circumstances in which reading from a manuscript is the most effective and advisable course. It is the surest way to avoid being misunderstood or misquoted. If you are on television or radio, reading is the best way of staying within your prescribed time. Most public addresses of government and association officials are read for these reasons.

You can inject spontaneity into your reading by interpolating an occasional spur-of-the-moment remark. You open with an introduction designed to relax your audience and capture attention. Then begin to read. When you come to a place where you need a story or example to illustrate your point, this should be merely indicated on your manuscript. Then ad-lib your anecdote. It will sound much more natural this way.

Joseph Martin of Massachusetts, former Speaker of the House of Representatives, says that congressmen follow a practice of having their speech manuscript typed in all capitals, triple-spaced. Triple spacing, however, means more paper to handle.

Before you deliver your speech, go through your script and underscore the words and phrases you want to emphasize. These markings will catch your eye in time to lead you into emphasis at the right point.

How to Read Aloud

No one should read a speech who is not a good reader. What do we mean by a good reader? One who speaks loudly enough to be heard in all parts of the room or hall. One who enunciates his vowels clearly and who doesn't hiss his consonants or trail off to a whisper at the end of a sentence. One who places stress where it belongs. The best-written speech will be a dud if read in a deadly monotone, as though the speaker merely had a job to do and was getting it over with. Use a conversational tone for the body of a speech that you read. But vary it when you come to declamatory passages, scriptural or poetic quotations, and moments of solemn warning or appeal.

Of the atrocious habit of ending sentences inaudibly, Sir Christopher Wren, architect and builder of St. Paul's Cathedral in London, once remarked that a preacher of average voice power might easily be heard 50 feet in front,

20 feet behind, and 30 feet on either side—provided he did not drop his voice at the end of a sentence.

Don't keep your eyes glued to your manuscript if you want to establish real rapport with your audience. In fact, aim at looking toward your listeners more than half the time. Instead of turning the sheets, simply slide them into another pile. No doubt you've heard speeches delivered so well this way that you could hardly tell whether the speaker had a manuscript before him.

You learn to read a speech well only through practice. Practice for enunciation, accented words, pauses, pronunciation. If a sentence is a question, be sure it is spoken as a question. If it's an exclamation, read it in exclamatory tones. Check the dictionary on every word about which you have the slightest doubt as to meaning or pronunciation.

Never repeat the same speech without reviewing to see if you need to make changes to fit the audience or the march of time. I've heard some ludicrous slips because this had not been done, such as addressing Lions when before an Optimists club or referring to a recently deceased person as though he were still among the living.

"You don't need to feel ashamed of having a script in front of you when you are speaking," says the Royal Bank of Canada in one of its *Monthly Letters*. "Your audience will not object, because your thoughtfulness in preparation makes it easier for them to follow your address." The fact that a speaker has gone to some trouble to organize his thinking on a subject adds impressiveness to the occasion. It leads the listeners to expect to hear the carefully considered views of the speaker and not something tossed off on impulse.

The Formal Speech from Notes

Granting everything that has been said in favor of some speakers' on some occasions reading their script, it must still be admitted that the highest form of the forensic art is the speech that is written out in full and then so well anchored in the speaker's mind that he can deliver it from a minimum of topical notes.

Some good speakers follow the same outline from which the speech was written. Others prefer a much more condensed or skeleton form for their notes, reducing them to about five or six main heads and several subheads under the divisions. These are typed on 3 by 5 or 4 by 6 inch cards that can be carried easily in a coat pocket or a handbag.

One Toastmaster says he does best by typing the opening phrases of all his key paragraphs, in order, on his cards. This is sufficient to recall to him the text that follows. He memorizes the points rather than the words to convey his ideas. He "talks" it through first to himself and then tries it alone out loud.

Memory Aids

"I had a good speech planned, but I forgot some of my best points and illustrations." Perhaps you've said something like this to yourself in that painful retrospection that often follows speechmaking. What kinds of memory prods can be used to prompt yourself?

Recalling anything depends upon the frequency, recency, and intensity with which you have contemplated or used it. A speech becomes easier to deliver in full the oftener you have delivered it. If you gave it only last week, the points are still fresh in your memory. And if you're interested enough in the subject to have studied it intensely, your recollection is further reinforced.

Many of us have been embarrassed by those memory blocks when the mind goes blank on some point. What to do in such a case? In conversation one can stop and ask, "Where was I?" But a public lapse is an unhappy experience. Here are two suggestions for meeting the situation.

1. Keep a card handy in your pocket, and at such a moment take it out and appear to read from it. This diversion will give you a breathing spell to collect your thoughts and eliminate the possibility of your staring at the audience, saying nothing. Looking at the card will give you time to remember what you started to say or else to concoct a fill-in remark.

Of course a woman can't keep cards in her pocket if her dress has no pockets, but this situation was solved by Mrs. Helen Miller, an able lecturer, who told me that she carries her three by five card notes to the lectern in a large manila file folder. Mrs. Miller decided that if she could not hide her notes, she would exploit them. The folder gave the impression that she was prepared to support her talk with substantial documentation. Laid on the lectern, it was unobtrusive but comfortingly available if needed.

2. Another solution of a memory lapse is to restate in different words the thought you have just expressed. Nearly always this brings to mind what you planned to say next. Previous preparation and subconscious association of ideas will rescue you.

An acquaintance of mine relates this experience.
I often get a warning flash from inside that says, "This word or name that you're going to use, you've forgotten." When that

happens, and I start consciously trying to fish up the term, it's usually futile. I've learned to plow around the obstacle by dropping the sentence if there is yet time, or using some synonym or general term such as "a great French philosopher," when I've forgotten the philosopher's name.

Some writers and speakers have devised various memory stunts and formulas. But it is safer not to clutter the mind with such tricks. Stick to natural associations and the frequency-recency-intensity rule.

Try It Out on the Dog

This heading is not meant to cast any reflection on those good wives and husbands who are asked to be the test audience for their spouses' oratory. They also serve. If they are critical they can do much to help perfect a speech.

Every theatergoer has an admiration for competent stage stars. How can the actor who plays Hamlet or Cyrano ever remember all his lines and make believe so realistically that you love or hate the character?

Well, we know that actors and actresses and singers, as a profession, are not superior in intellectual faculties to practitioners of many other vocations. They attain their spellbinding effects through laborious, never-ending rehearsals. There is no better formula for a speaker—if he starts out with something in his mind worth saying.

One way to rehearse is to hand the manuscript to your wife or husband and ask her or him to make a note of points you omit as you speak. When you've finished, review these omissions. Then go over the speech again; but this time your listener makes notes of flaws in delivery. This second run-through is the point at which to time yourself.

Rehearsing a speech the first time or two may seem a deadly affair. You'll be oppressed with a feeling that "this is going to be a flop." The main reason is that speaking without benefit of a multiple audience takes all the excitement and inspiration out of it. For a really effective rehearsal, get yourself keyed up to a tension resembling that of the real thing. Stand on your feet behind a table that simulates a lectern. Pitch your voice as though you were in front of an audience. Ask your critic not to stop you but to make notes of all you will discuss when you've concluded. The very act of hearing your own voice speaking tends to fix your points in mind because it enlists another sense organ: your ears.

Sometimes the rehearsal will show that there is really something wrong with your speech—a flaw that can be corrected. A husband and wife had collaborated in writing a speech in which they were to relate their experiences as a writing team. The plan was that both would be on the platform and would speak alternately, each for three stretches of about five minutes. A rehearsal showed this scheme to be cumbersome and artificial. They changed it to have the husband lead off for ten minutes, then the wife to come in for fifteen minutes, and the husband to wind up with a five-minute conclusion. That gave them a chance to divide the subject more conveniently and not to be bouncing to and from the mike too often. "The joint speech went over well," the husband told me. "But without rehearsing we would have followed the original plan and failed. Of that I'm convinced."

One can read a poem a hundred times, routinely, and not memorize it. The memorizing is achieved by repeating as much of it as you can, then looking at the copy to prompt yourself, and trying again. Conscious effort must go into any memory exercise. After it is perfected, you do it unconsciously. Some older men have the faculty of recalling verses they have not read or thought of since their school or college days. But in the beginning it is through drilling that they fastened the lines in mind.

Psychologists suggest that the best way to memorize speech materials is to review them just before going to sleep at night. Once the speech is firmly in mind, it is a good idea not to read anything on a related subject until after it has been delivered. Any impressions thus acquired would tend to fuse with previous notes and make it more difficult for you to remember and identify your factual sources.

A Last Word

Do not lose sight of the fact that the purpose of your speech is to convey your message to your listeners. Any method that helps you do this is useful; any method that interferes with your communication is to be avoided. Whether you use notes or memorize or read your speech, practice will increase your effectiveness.

Summary

Become familiar with all the various techniques of public speaking.

Make Short Impromptu Speeches

1. When you are called on for a comment on any discussion.

2. When you hear a flagrant bit of misinformation or propaganda and feel an urge to refute it.

3. When a subject is under discussion on which you have pertinent information not generally available.

Make Extemporaneous Speeches

1. When you lack the time to write your text in detail.

2. When the subject is one on which you are sufficiently informed so that little research is necessary and all you'll need is some notes, organized for reference as you speak or carried in the memory.

Make Formal Speeches

1. When the subject or the occasion makes it important that you be quite explicit and not misunderstood or misquoted.

2. To say more in a limited time than you could in any other way.

Choose your own best technique for presenting a formal speech:

1. Reading the speech, but only if you're a good reader.

2. Speaking from brief notes made from your script:

(*a*) To save the labor and avoid the hazards of memorizing a whole speech.

(*b*) To remind yourself of the main points to be covered.

(*c*) To give your presentation the color of spontaneity and informality.

The most effective way to learn to speak effectively is to speak and receive evaluation of your efforts. A Toastmasters club provides frequent opportunities to practice all kinds of delivery before helpful listeners.

CHAPTER 6

How to Organize Your Speech

A BUILDER needs to follow a blueprint to convert bricks, wood, and glass into a finished building; a speaker needs to follow an outline to convert an appealing subject, stimulating ideas, and research material into a speech.

You cannot built a house by making the back steps, then the second floor, and then the first floor. Neither can you create a speech by making your points in haphazard sequence. The audience will have difficulty in following disconnected thoughts.

A speech outline is a blueprint to help you organize your material and present it in a sequence that will produce the desired effect on your audience. This will make it easy for the listener to follow and to remember. It enables you to build point on point to achieve the emotional impact or reasoned conclusion that will induce the audience reaction you seek.

What an Outline Does for You

An outline is the simplest and best way to organize your talk.

1. It compels you to analyze your argument and to examine your supporting materials, selecting only the best and placing these in the most advantageous spots.

2. It reveals any gaps or flaws in your reasoning and in the development of your points.

3. It makes it easier for you to remember what you want to say and to deliver with a minimum reliance on notes or manuscript.

4. It enables you to get the most out of your points because you will present them in a natural or orderly sequence, reaching a climax without omitting essentials or distracting the audience with digressions.

How to Organize Your Outline

Write your subject on a card or a sheet of paper. Under your subject, write the audience purpose: what you want your audience to know, think, feel, or do as a result of hearing your speech. Put this material in front of you, with room to stack closer to you the material you have collected.

Your speech is going to have an introduction, a body, and a conclusion. Sort your material into three corresponding piles.

Read the material in each stack and make a list of the *points* you want to make in each of the three sections of your speech. Then sort the material that supports each of the points and stack the material under each of the points to which it relates. Summarize each point in a brief sentence. Write under it a brief line summarizing the supporting facts or other material.

If your list indicates that you have two main points in your introduction, three main points in the body of your speech, and one concluding point, you should have six stacks of material in front of you. If some of your notes won't go into any of the piles, you have these alternatives:

1. Discard the material that won't group because it is irrelevant to your purpose or the points you want to make.

2. If you have too many unclassified notes, either your main points are not broad enough and need restatement or you are in danger of obscuring them by trying to make too many lesser points. Discard the minor points.

How to Group Your Points

You have now determined your main points and decided whether they belong in your opening, the main part of your speech, or its conclusion. Next, you need to work out the order in which you will present them.

Remember that your aim is to carry the audience with you to the conclusion you would like them to reach. You want them to understand your points and to remember them. While lawyers arguing in support of a legal brief will attempt to present their points in logical order, it is usually preferable for speakers to rely on a natural sequence. Natural sequence utilizes the psychologically sound principle of association of ideas, which may or may not be logical but is the way most people's minds work.

Chronological Order or Time Sequence

Any narrative or descriptive presentation can usually be handled best by using a time sequence in arranging the points. You want your listeners to say to themselves, "And *then* what did you do?" Whether you talk about your visit to the zoo or how to build a birdhouse, they will follow you and remember what you have said if you take them step by step in the order of what you do.

Time sequence is also useful in treating the historical development of a subject. For example, if your title were "Can We Civilize Warfare?" you might refer first to some of the battles related in the Bible, then speak of the code of chivalry in the Middle Ages, and proceed to discuss the attempts to formulate a fabric of international law, bringing in the stories of Florence Nightingale, Clara Barton, the Sanitary Commission in the Civil War, the formation of the International Red Cross, the Geneva Convention, and the efforts to establish treaties as a result of the destruction of Hiroshima.

The Spatial Order

If your talk requires you to create pictures or visual images in the minds of your listeners, you will be referring to geographic or dimensional matters, and spatial sequence will be suitable for your purpose.

For example, in relating your visit to the Library of

Congress you would probably take your audience with you, picturing what you saw in the order in which you saw it. You might describe the imposing west façade, with its bronze fountain and classical figures, which you pass as you enter the building. Then you might continue with your impression of the central stairs and the beautiful Corinthian columns and move on to the first-floor reading room—and so through the building, perhaps reaching a climax at the exhibit of the original of the Constitution, whose guaranties of free expression made possible the fine library.

As in the caption of a newspaper picture, you may list your points from left to right, from top to bottom, or from near to far.

Order of Importance

Here you have a choice of starting with points of lesser value and building to a climax, or of opening with an attention-arresting point and following it with others of lesser importance. If you follow the latter sequence, something should be held back in order not to limp off the platform at your conclusion with an anticlimax.

This is a highly adaptable sequence. You may organize your points by going from the primitive to the most modern, the simple to the complex, the smallest to the largest, the cheapest to the most expensive, or any similar pattern that your audience will recognize and can use as an easy way to recall your message.

The system you use should help you achieve your audience purpose. This is the test that dictates which sequence to follow in developing your outline.

Problem and Solution

If you are consulting this book because you are a business or professional man and your desire to talk in public springs from political, economic, or civic problems you want to do something about, the cause-and-effect sequence will be of much value to you. In its simplest and most generally applicable form, here it is:

1. State the problem.
2. Tell why it is important and how much it matters to your listeners.
3. State, briefly, other solutions that have been offered or tried. Then explain why they did not or will not work.
4. Offer your solution as the correct one.
5. Present your arguments supporting your solution.
6. Tell the audience what they can do to bring about your solution.

Or, the nature of your subject may require that you first state the facts, then describe the problem arising from the facts, and finally discuss your proposal for solving the problem.

If the subject is familiar to your listeners, such as "The Local School Problem," you have a choice. You may state your proposition (more funds should or should not be appropriated); then marshal the points supporting your proposal. Or, you may start with your arguments and then show how they lead you to the conclusion that funds should or should not be raised. In each instance, you must decide whether to state your opinion and support it or to cite facts and reasons that lead you to your opinion.

Beginnings

The initial impression you give your audience is so important that you should single it out for special attention. In preparing your outline, write the points you want to put across in your opening. Many experienced speakers prepare the body of their talk first and then go back and prepare the stage setting and the finale. This is good procedure; it assures a closely knit relation between all three segments of the talk. After all, you cannot decide how to lead into your subject until you know what you want to lead into.

Your opening should arrest the attention of your audience. It should draw their thoughts away from those that preoccupied them and get them all thinking about your subject. In my classes and with Toastmasters, I have found the "P A I L" formula to be a helpful guide.

P—*Present* yourself to your audience. If you have confidence in your ability to make pertinent, witty, pleasing, informal remarks, allow yourself a few minutes—but very few—to make them here.

This is also the time when you will wish to acknowledge your introduction. The chairman will probably have presented you with several laudatory comments. You will wish to say something to show you do not take this tribute too seriously. If the audience greets you with applause, simply smile or nod. The main thing is to set a pleasantly relaxed mood.

As for the opening sentence, addressing your audience, there is no set form. "Ladies and Gentlemen" is usually appropriate, though for a class reunion or picnic, "Friends," or "Folks" would be better. In speaking before a club of which you are not a member, something on the order of "Kiwanians and Guests" is always proper.

A—*Arrest* audience attention. Your attention-getting statement must be strong enough to convert your audience into willing listeners. This statement is closely tied to the next point.

I—*Interest* your audience. Audience attention will stray unless you give listeners a reason for staying with you. One technique is to start with a challenging question. Another is to use a short but lively story. A third is to open with an attention-arresting comment. For example, traffic safety is not a very exciting subject in itself. However, you can capture your audience with a shock statement and relate this to their interest in the subject with one sentence such as "If you are a parent with two children, you can expect that one of them will be involved in a traffic accident before he grows up."

L—*Lead* into the body of your talk. After the sentence above, capitalize on your listeners' interest by saying, perhaps, "I want to tell you what you can do to reduce your children's chances of becoming traffic statistics."

Some Things Not to Do When Opening Your Speech

Don't try to greet all the notables present. "Mr. Chairman, Mayor Buckle, Dr. Beech, Rev. Mr. Waddell, Senator Jackson, Ladies and Gentlemen!" is pompous and wholly unnecessary except possibly in the case of a high political aspirant speaking before a really distinguished audience. If you feel it would be a good gesture to call any names of those present, bring them into the body of the speech.

Don't state the title of your speech in the opening. Use

those moments for something more impressive. Feed them a bit of suspense.

Don't open your speech with any kind of apology. It defeats your purpose; it gets hearers listening for weaknesses instead of merits. "Never explain," was a rule of Elbert Hubbard's. "Your friends don't need it and your enemies won't believe you anyway." Or, as someone else has said, "Don't talk about your shortcomings; they'll discover them soon enough."

Don't go into an explanation of "When your chairman asked me to speak here..."

Don't thresh over your difficulty in choosing a subject. Let the audience believe you're discussing something of such overwhelming interest that there was never for a moment any doubt as to what you wanted to talk about.

Endings

The ending of a speech is like the roof of a house; it can't save a weak structure but it may conceal some sins. Since your conclusion provides your audience with their final impression, you will want to give this part of your speech some extra polish.

Your closing statements should be brief; they should be closely related to your audience purpose; and they should let your listeners know you are finished. It is possible to be brief without being abrupt. "What do I want them to think about as they leave?" may help you to select your closing comments. If you have not put across your ideas in the body of your talk, it is too late to do it in your conclusion. This is not a second chance; it is an opportunity to emphasize and to fix in the listeners' minds the message you have already put across—to make clear what you want of your listeners.

There are six major methods for concluding your talk. Because your closing remarks are your final opportunity to reach your audience, do not leave them to chance or the inspiration of the moment. You cannot afford to fumble or to be inconclusive.

1. *Direct appeal.* If your audience purpose is to get your listeners to do something, this is an effective method. You have told them what you want them to do and why they should do it; now you nail it down by asking them to act. One way of making such an appeal is by waking emotion or by voicing a rousing declaration or challenge.

2. *Quotation.* An appropriate quotation may conclude many kinds of talks by providing a graceful ending, and it has additional values that recommend it. It is a form of appeal to a higher source. You borrow the prestige and influence of an established authority on your subject to reassure your listeners that you are not alone in what you ask them to think, feel, or do. Those whose statements are quotable usually have a gift for expression, and you may find one ringing sentence that summarizes all that you have said in an easy-to-remember form. Such a brief quotation also serves to crystallize the thinking of the audience.

3. *Summary.* If the purpose of your talk has been to inform or to convince your listeners, the summary will be valuable in reviewing briefly your major steps. This will fix your points with each listener, and by restating your ideas in different words you may reach minds that did not respond to your fuller presentation. Be careful not to repeat yourself at length. Audiences do not like to be pushed

by a speaker who is too insistent or who tries to drill them in what to think.

4. *Look ahead.* If the purpose and subject of your talk is to stimulate your listeners' concern for the future, you may want to close with a prediction. You may hold forth hope and the promise of better things to come, or you may warn of disastrous consequences. In either event you turn the thoughts of your audience to the future.

5. *Ask a rhetorical question.* Questions are useful for opening a speech because the audience expects your talk to provide answers. However, the rhetorical question that does not call for or expect an answer may be used as a means of inducing your audience to think of their own answer—if your talk has made clear the answer you want them to give.

The rhetorical question may be combined with other methods of closing. If your talk, for example, has championed a bond issue for new schools, you may summarize the points for the bond issue briefly, then turn your listeners' thoughts to the future and the consequences of their vote decision, ending with a question: "If you vote against this bond issue your children will sit in classrooms that grow more crowded and unhealthy with each passing year; your children will get less from their lessons. Is this the educational opportunity you want to give your children?"

6. *Refer to your opening comments.* Some talks do not require a summary, an appeal, or a prediction. If you have reported a trip or an experience of interest to your listeners, none of these conclusions may be appropriate. All that is required is to let your audience know you are finished and that you have done what you set out to do. A reference to your opening will tie up with your talk, just as

Q.E.D. or *Quod erat demonstrandum* is used by mathematicians at the end of their solution of a problem—"which was to be demonstrated." It's not a bad idea to ask yourself, as you finish your outline, whether you have made such a demonstration.

How to Time Your Speech

In organizing your talk, it is important to keep in mind the time allotted to you. If you have not been told, ask. Time is an important element in the success of any program. It is better to have your talk run a little under the time limit than over it.

There are three ways to avoid time trouble: (1) in preparing your speech, keep it within the time limit; (2) make your speech flexible so you can omit sections easily; (3) don't speed your delivery to say more in the time allowed.

Timing Begins When You Prepare Your Talk

Let's say that when you were invited to speak it was agreed that you would have thirty minutes. How long should your speech be?

Most of us talk at the rate of about 125 words a minute, with 140 to 150 words a minute as the upper limit. If you plan to read a thirty-minute speech, it should run to about 3,750 words in length. This is approximately twelve pages of double-spaced typewritten sheets, if you use standard manuscript margins and the usual 8½ by 11-inch paper.

However, if you plan to speak from notes, you will need more time to cover the subject as you have written it, or you will need to cut your material a little. When you speak extemporaneously, you probably speak more slowly than when you read from a manuscript. You also tend to elaborate on your illustrative material. Therefore, as a practical matter a written text of 3,000 to 3,300 words is enough for a thirty-minute speech given from notes.

After the first draft of your speech has been written, read it aloud as nearly as possible like your intended delivery. This first check against the allotted time will indicate how much condensing, omitting, or rewriting will be required.

Now shorten your speech a little more, to allow time for your acknowledgment of the introduction and for any extemporaneous remarks at the opening that may be suggested to you by circumstances or by something said by the person who introduced you. If you expect to receive applause during your talk, make allowance for that also.

Use a Watch

The only way to be reasonably sure about the length of your talk is to rehearse it with a watch at hand. Whether you plan to read your speech or deliver it from notes on cards, rehearse it two or three times, and in pencil make marginal notations at several points as a guide to elapsed time. For a thirty-minute speech, you may want to mark "15" in red pencil at the halfway mark and "25" when you have five minutes to go.

Make It Flexible

Everyone who does much speaking is certain sooner or later to run into that trying situation in which he is robbed of some of his time. You're to have thirty minutes, and adjournment time is one-thirty. At one o'clock the chairman whispers that he has a couple of announcements to get out of the way and then you're on. However, after fifteen anxious minutes, during which you listen to a brother extol the local Boys' Club Pancake Roundup, a report on the size of the fish caught at last week's Fishing Derby, and a windy announcement of a coming Square Dance Festival, the chairman turns to you with a whispered apology and asks if you would mind talking only twenty minutes.

To a conscientious speaker who made two trips to the public library to do research and gave up a Sunday putting a thirty-minute speech in order, such a request is as if a veterinarian were to ask you if it makes much difference if he crops your pup's tail just between the hip bones. You are suddenly asked to crop one-third of your precious speech. With some advance notice you could reorganize your outline and make it; now all you can do is amputate.

There is a way out of this impasse: anticipate its possibility when you write your speech. Put it together in such a way that one or more topics can be dropped without much damage to your main theme. Make a marginal note of the time required to deliver each topic, and make a mental note of the section or sections that can be omitted in case of emergency.

If there are three major points in the body of your talk and each of them takes seven minutes to deliver, you will have to decide whether you can omit one point without referring to it at all or whether you can summarize the point in one or two minutes, explaining that time prevents you from dealing with it in detail. If the point is so important that its complete omission will detract substantially from the effectiveness of your speech, choose to summarize it. You have cooperated with the chairman if you cut your speech from thirty minutes to twenty-two minutes instead of reducing it to twenty minutes.

Don't Speed Up

Although the foregoing suggestion will not enhance your effectiveness, it will minimize the damage. You are, as it were, retreating to prepared points. It is better than attempting a drastic editing job while the chairman is introducing you. And it is far better than the alternative usually attempted by inexperienced speakers. Asked to reduce their thirty-minute talk to twenty minutes, they often try to talk faster, to crowd the thirty-minute talk into the shorter period. This is a good way to ruin the entire presentation.

Sometimes it happens that while speaking from notes you are carried away by what you are saying and take longer than you had planned in making your point, because you have added material extemporaneously. In this event, at some stage in your talk you notice that you are running substantially over the time you have allowed yourself. You will be aware of this because you will have schooled yourself to glance at your watch unobtrusively at two or three stations along the way.

You cannot switch abruptly from your normal rate of speaking to an accelerated pace without seriously marring your effect. Using the method I have described, you can omit one or two points or slip over them with a brief summary, and your audience will never know the difference. Time your topics, and decide in advance which you can drop if necessary.

Summary

An outline will aid you in building a speech that will accomplish its purposes and will help your listeners to get the most out of it.

To organize your outline, write your purposes and your subject, then place your materials in separate piles for your opening, body, and conclusion. Discard any material that does not relate to your purposes.

Define your major points for each of the three parts of your speech. Group pertinent supporting material with each point.

Select the sequence best suited to your subject and purpose and arrange the points with their supplemental material in proper order.

The major sequences are:

1. Chronological: arrangement of points in order of time.
2. Spatial: dimensional or visual sequence of points.
3. Order of importance.
4. Problem solution: state the problem, your solution, and the points supporting it; or state the solution and then list your points in the order that leads to it inescapably.

Prepare the outline of the body of your talk; then plan the opening that will lead into it effectively. Your opening should establish a pleasant, receptive relationship with your audience, focus their attention on your subject, interest them, and lead them into your main points. Avoid any attempt to greet all the notables present, to apologize, or to describe any difficulties you had in preparing your speech.

Your conclusion should be brief and related to your audience purpose; it should let your listeners know you are finished. You can (1) make a direct appeal, (2) end with a quotation, (3) summarize your points, (4) look to the future, (5) ask a rhetorical question, or (6) refer to your opening remarks.

In organizing your speech to the specified time limit, it is important to keep the allotted time in mind as you write, rehearse with a watch, and make the speech flexible enough so that if you find you must shorten the talk you will know in advance which sections might be cut down or even omitted.

Your outline is your road map to guide you and your audience to your destination. Your method of arranging the points in your outline is the route you choose to travel to your destination.

CHAPTER 7

How to Write Your Speech

LIKE the skilled athlete who gauges his development and training to bring him to peak condition on the day of his performance, you have been preparing gradually for the moment you will be at your best: when you advance to the lectern and address your audience.

You have selected your subject, determined the purpose of your speech, listed your ideas and the points you want to put across, organized an outline, and completed the research. In fact, you have done everything but put your speech in final form. What is the best way to capitalize on all your preparation?

I subscribe to the judgment of the best practitioners of the art of public speaking: write your speech. If you want to give the best performance of which you are capable, write your speech—and rewrite it, if necessary—until you have it exactly as you hope to deliver it. Whether you use the written text on the platform and how to use it are separate subjects discussed in Chapter 5.

Here are the main reasons why you should write your speech.

1. Written discourse is more precise than oral expression. If you write exactly what you intend to say, the right words are more likely to come to mind on the platform, whether you read them or remember them; you are not so apt to fumble. In handling controversial subjects on which you don't want to be misquoted, a written text is a protective device.

2. When you have written your speech completely, you are in a better position to study it for organization and expression. You have a "second chance," at home alone, to make revisions that enable you to say more in the time allotted and say it better—without anyone being the wiser.

3. A written manuscript can be underscored for the words, phrases, and sentences that you wish to emphasize. Pauses, rising inflections, and other helpful vocal effects can be indicated and practiced.

4. Your opus is on record for future use in other speaking engagements or for publication.

Speech versus Essay

When you write your speech, remember one essential point: You must *listen* to what you write. How will it *sound* to your listeners? Writing that is to be spoken must appeal to the ear. It takes most people a little more time to comprehend what they *hear* than what they *read*. It is more difficult for them to concentrate. Your speed of delivery, therefore, affects their ability to get what you say. On the other hand, your tone, your inflection, your timing and emphasis, supply aids to understanding that people do not have when they read the printed word.

The words you use and the way you use them are different when you speak. The audience cannot pause over an arresting or difficult sentence and go back to reread it. Therefore, when you write a speech you must constantly be aware that you are writing words that you will speak, not words your audience will read.

Let us consider some of the differences that distinguish a speech in style, expression, and delivery from an essay or magazine article.

Getting from One Topic to Another

Transitions to bridge the gaps in switching from one topic to another must be made much more obvious in a speech. Unless you take this precaution, listeners who are not alert will tend to jump to the conclusion that you're still referring to Topic A when in fact you are well launched on Topic B. What the writer attains through typographical divisions the speaker must effect vocally.

Alexander Hamilton's speeches were notable for his clean-cut transitions. In his addresses that have been preserved we find frequently such remarks as these:

Without dwelling any longer on this subject, I shall proceed to the question immediately before the committee....

But, dismissing these reflections, let us examine....

I now proceed to consider the objection with regard to the number of representatives, as it now stands....

Style More Conversational

In writing an article you might include such a "written" sentence as this: "His thinking is analytic, penetrating, illuminating, and conclusive." The same thought would be driven home with more impact in a speech if you cut it up into short, forceful sentences that sound the way you would in private conversation: "His thinking is analytic. It's penetrating. It's illuminating. It's conclusive."

Short, simple sentences with key words repeated add force to speech but seem contrived in written presentations. In his first address to the joint session of Congress, President Lyndon B. Johnson (as recorded by the *New York Times*) used the speaker's style of writing with great effectiveness: "The need is here. The need is now. I ask your help. We meet in grief, but let us also meet in renewed dedication and renewed vigor. Let us meet in action, in tolerance and in mutual understanding."

Indirect beginnings, such as "In accordance with this idea," should be made more direct. "To carry out this idea" is stronger. Use active in preference to passive verbs. "The assignment was given our committee to..." should be changed to "You directed our committee to...." Use the first person rather than the third person. "I believe" is more authoritative than "It is believed." A word of warning, though: Be careful not to punctuate your speech with too many I's or me's.

In writing a speech, keep constantly in mind that you will be standing before your audience and talking *to* them, not *at* them. As you write a sentence, ask yourself, "Is this the way I talk? Does it sound in character for me? Does it get me as close as possible to these people?" A speech is not the same as conversation, but it should be much more conversational than an essay.

Those Little Remarks in Parenthesis

Parenthetical expressions are generally offensive to the trained writer, but they have a place in a speech. Sentences such as the following from notes made of a political speech by Senator Thruston Morton would seem quite awkward in type.

I'm speaking as a Kentuckian (I salute the delegation from Arkansas: thank God for Arkansas; it keeps Kentucky from being at the bottom of the lists of economic statistics by states), but I want to talk about what's good for the whole country, North, South, East and West.

The aside was introduced in a tone of sympathetic levity that drew a laugh without detracting from the speaker's serious thought.

At a PTA meeting I heard a mother speak on the subject of helping the children with their homework. She interspersed her serious talk with parenthetical and apparently impromptu references to her daughter's puzzlement over the square of the hypotenuse and her husband's transparently lame efforts to conceal his ignorance of the historic significance of the date 1066 A.D. These asides struck a responsive chord in every listener who had been confronted by similar cultural crises, and the bonds with her audience were firmly established.

Your parenthetical references can add a warm, human touch that will make your speech more effective and strengthen your ties with your audience. However, do not rely entirely on the inspiration of the moment. Recently a young grade school teacher gave her first talk before my public speaking class. Her subject was herself. At one point she commented on the problem of raising a family and teaching school. She said, "My husband and I have three children...," then as an impromptu afterthought, parenthetically (and unnecessarily), she added, "We like to do things together." She brought down the house.

Go Easy on Figures

It should hardly be necessary to warn even an amateur speaker to be abstemious in his use of statisics. And yet I heard an economics professor, who talked on Civil War financing, ladle out an indigestible mass of statistics on bond issues, revenue collections, Treasury notes, and appropriations, all down to the last dollar. He even insisted on interlarding his speech with exact dates on every act, Union and Confederate. His audience soon dozed off.

"Shun statistics as you would a creditor," says Paul Jones, the speaker who did so much in his job with the National Safety Council to keep people from maiming and killing themselves. Mr. Jones was, of course, exaggerating for emphasis. You *can* use statistics in a speech, but unless you translate, dramatize, or visualize them you will merely bore your audience. The type of visualization represented by laying all the hot dogs consumed in a year end to end and spanning the earth with them fourteen times has been worn rather thin. An ingenious speaker will find less trite and more effective ways of illustrating a nine-digit statistic.

Use statistics only to submit or prove a point. Use as few as will suffice to put over the point or occasionally to elaborate it. Never use them just to impress an audience with your scholarship. The same rule, incidentally, applies to poetical quotations, classical allusions, foreign words and phrases, and technical terms.

Clarity—the First Objective

Clarity must be your primary objective in writing and delivering a speech. Unless you make yourself understood, your speech is worthless. The most you can expect from audiences is sympathetic attention as you start talking. It is your responsibility to catch and hold their interest so they will *listen* to you and not merely *hear* you. To do this, you must make sure they understand clearly what you are saying.

If your ideas are foggy in your own mind, obviously you cannot communicate them clearly to others. Listening, like public speaking, is a cultivated skill. Since most people do not know how to listen effectively and do not hear the same ideas you are expressing, you must be so clear in your choice of words that you minimize the work of your audience in understanding you.

When I asked the members of my advanced public speaking class at California State College at Fullerton to write in one or two sentences the main ideas they had wanted to get across in their speeches, the results were disconcerting for about seven out of every ten students. Each discovered that his main point, as the class understood it, was quite different from that he had written in advance and thought his speech expressed. Also, they all discovered that the words used in writing their main points did not convey the same ideas to their listeners that the speakers had in mind.

Bill, an employee, is talking with his boss. The boss says, "I think, Bill, that this is the best way to do your job." Bill says, "Oh, yeah?" Is Bill agreeing with his boss, expressing hurt feelings, or indicating that he disagrees with his boss? We all think we know what "Oh, yeah" means. F. J. Roethlisberger, one of the outstanding authorities on communications, in a speech delivered at Northwestern University's Centennial Conference on Communications, said that Bill and his boss were miles apart and that "Oh, yeah" meant different opinions and feelings for each.

"You stammer in speech because you falter in thought," the noted British Labour Party leader Aneurin Bevan once told his followers. "If you can't say it, you don't know it."

Keep on asking yourself the question, "Can this be interpreted in more than one way?" If the answer is "Yes," rewrite the passage because someone is sure to get the wrong meaning, even if he has to torture your words to do it.

One of the best definitions of good writing was expressed by Dwight Morrow: "Good English can be recognized by a simple test. Is this sentence simple and precise?" Morrow added that this is all one needs to worry about in his English. The wordy speaker is the fuzzy thinker. "I cannot hear you because of what you are saying."

"Simplify, Simplify, Simplify!"

Clarity is usually enhanced by simplicity. All experts on writing advise us to make it simple. This is good counsel, but it is often misunderstood. What seems simple and direct in hearing or reading is usually far from simple in planning. Rather, simplicity is one of the finest arts in writing, to be learned slowly and with practice. When the paragraph labors, the writer has not. The height of art is to conceal art.

Here are a few points to watch in simplifying your style when writing a speech.

1. *Get right into your subject.* Don't spar around with lengthy introductions and whereases.

2. *Use short words wherever possible.* In the case of long words, stop and ask yourself if a shorter word can be substituted without loss of precision.

3. *Shorten your sentences.* Put periods in place of some of the "ands" or semicolons.

Rudolph Flesch, in his book *The Art of Readable Writing*, tells us that clarity is related to the length of words and the length of sentences. An average sentence of five to ten words Mr. Flesch rates as easy to understand; fifteen-word sentences are standard; and sentences of more than fifteen words are usually difficult.

4. *Use as few adjectives and adverbs as you can.* A heavy sprinkling of modifiers weakens what you say. The real pulse of speech is in the verbs we use.

5. *Qualify as few statements as possible.* No "on the other hand," "if," "but. . . ." Some exceptions are necessary in the interest of accuracy, but you pay a price for them in effect.

6. *Be sparing* in your use of the participial "ing" form of the verb. One trade journal editor won't stand for a headline such as "Running a Meeting." He insists on the infinitive form, "How to Run a Meeting."

7. *Use the active* rather than the passive voice wherever possible, as we have noted before, and personal pro-

nouns in preference to the third person. Avoid such jargon as the following: "I do not anticipate the realization of the presently proposed orbital passenger flights until a very much later date in time, when I expect them to become a reality." The speaker must have meant that "I don't think we're going to get a man into space right away, but I'm pretty sure we shall have one there before long."

Color—the Second Objective

Your manuscript may be carefully organized, a model of clear, simplified diction, and yet lack one of the prime ingredients of a good speech. It can be dull. While thinking about grammar, clarity, and simplicity you must not forget the other element: color. Color carries that hard-to-define quality of impact.

Make the Most of Your Vocabulary

One of the best ways of adding color to your speech is through the correct imaginative use of words. A good vocabulary will allow you to express common thoughts in an uncommon way. The proper use of words will also help you evoke the emotional response you desire from your audience.

Always try to use words exactly. If you use expressions without knowing precisely what they mean, you may tell your audience something other than what you intended. Also try to avoid pretentious usage. The weakness of words such as "fortuitous," "loquacious," "fustian," and "intone" is that they do not belong in the conversational vocabulary of most speakers. A good rule is never to use words simply to display your own learning.

How Much Vernacular or Slang?

An audience made up largely of young men, such as a sportsmen's group, will relish your speech all the more for an occasional slang expression. The best rule for using any form of the vernacular is this: if it seems in good taste for the occasion, and if you don't have to define the terms to your listeners, just the right amount will put life into your discourse. But slang expressions that have to be defined are too much like jokes that have to be explained. Neither is desirable in a speech.

Ways to Improve Your Language

Facility with words is acquired through reading and writing, listening and talking.

Although the rapid-reading experts frown on such interruptions, there is still no better way of adding to your stock of words than by reading serious books and magazines with a dictionary at your elbow. Every unfamiliar word should be a red flag that says, "Stop and look up meaning." This goes for unfamiliar names and places, also.

In conversation or in listening to speeches, try to make a mental note of effective words that you understand but have not been using. Then at the first opportunity put them into your speech or writing. Our words are like our muscles in one respect. Words seldom used become atrophied in the memory and are soon lost. The average person uses less than 10 per cent of the 500,000 words in the English language. There's room for you to expand.

Everyone who does much speaking needs a few reference works in his own desk library. The dictionary serves to spell and define words about which you are uncertain.

Equally valuable in writing speeches is a theasurus or word finder. It serves to locate the word of your choice to express a given thought. One of the best is *Roget's International Thesaurus of English Words and Phrases.* You start with a word in the area in which you are interested and look it up in the alphabetical vocabulary in the back of the book. This refers you to a numbered list of words relating to that subject.

You're trying to think of a particular and provocative adjective to describe a people who are quarrelsome and troublemaking. The word is buried in your consciousness, but you consult your thesaurus. In the alphabetical key in the back of the book you find *Warfare,* No. 722. Turning to 722 in numerical order, you see more than a page of words relating to war and warlike traits. For your purpose there are *unpacific, belligerent, combative, martial, bellicose.* The last-named is the word you want in this instance.

A book of synonyms helps in drawing fine distinctions among words that mean nearly the same thing but have certain connotations that you want to attain or avoid. You are uncertain about using *hypothesis* or *theory,* for example. *The Dictionary of Synonyms* tells you that to men of science there is a big difference between the two. A hypothesis is more tentative, less conclusive, than a theory. It has a scientific connotation not present in *theory,* which applies as well to religion, politics, or literature as to science.

There are times when you may want to consult a manual of English composition for the fine points of sentence structure. Reference works such as Fowler's *A Dictionary of Modern English Usage,* Nicholson's *Dictionary of Amer-*

ican-English Usage, based on the Fowler book, and *Write It Right,* by John B. Opdycke, are valuable. A good atlas is also helpful if you are going to deal with places in your talks.

Figurative Speech

The various figures of speech are tools that help a speech writer to add color because they accomplish two desirable ends: they help to clarify, and they provoke interest. The principal ones, familiar to all, are the simile and the metaphor. Others, less common but often employed, include allegory, antithesis, apostrophe, exclamation, hyperbole, irony, metonymy, personification, and synecdoche. For examples of each, consult your dictionary or any standard text on English composition.

I have said that clarity and color are of primary concern when you write your speech, and I have previously suggested ways to make your writing of words to be spoken clear and interesting. Let me emphasize two cautionary points.

1. While simplicity is the handmaiden of clarity, many speakers confuse *simplification* with *simplicity*. As Charles W. Ferguson states in his book, *Say It with Words,* "I construe the latter to be clarity with sweat, whereas simplification generally means taking some passage that is not very interesting to begin with and translating it into a species of baby talk."

2. Figures of speech will make your talk more interesting and more easily understood, but making pictures with words will not brighten or add color to your speech if you use wilted words. Avoid clichés or tired language. Don't be afraid to draw on your observation and imagination

for fresh pictures with which to explain your point in images familiar to your audience.

Ghost-Writing a Speech

Writing speeches for others to deliver has become a trade in its own right. Many top executives simply cannot find the time to prepare all the addresses they are called upon to deliver. As a consequence, numerous young people in business and government have risen rapidly because of their ability to express ideas and policies in speeches written for higher-echelon executives. This is one sure way to bring your mind and abilities to the attention of those who can give you recognition.

When you have the opportunity to draft a speech for somebody else, the first thing to bear in mind is the obvious but very important fact that you are writing for somebody else and not for yourself. Study your man. You must know his point of view and his style of speaking.

Toastmaster Clifford G. Massoth, a successful ghost writer, says in an article ("The Ghost of a Speaker," *The Toastmaster*, April, 1960) that he has found that a busy executive seldom has very definite ideas of what he wants to say. But he can give his assistant a general outline of the main thoughts he would like to leave with his audience. This is only a beginning for the writer. The second step, Massoth adds, is to go to some of the people in the organization before which your principal is to make the talk, tell them frankly what you are doing, and ask for material that will help in giving the audience what it expects of the speaker. However, if you use this approach you must be sure that the speaker does not mind admitting he is using a ghost. If you are at all uncertain on this point, it would be better to pose simply as a *researcher* on the speaker's behalf.

Edward Hegarty helped some of his associates at Westinghouse to write their speeches. He found a tendency on the part of executives before whom a text is placed to say, "This is good, but I wonder if it has the dignity I should have in addressing this group?" Hegarty believes the writer should try to sell his principal on forgetting about "dignity." After all, dignity is the main trouble with too many speeches. Even bankers or bishops like speeches with a flavor of color and individuality.

It would be a mistake, of course, to write a speech full of fire and brimstone and modern slang for a naturally reserved executive to deliver. Any speaker should stay "in character." Write as *he* might write, but *at his best*. Don't dress him up in starch as though he were filling a high-church pulpit, but let him appear more as he would on informal occasions when he's enjoying himself.

As a ghost writer you will find your usefulness extended if you try to forget pride of authorship. You are attempting the difficult task of placing yourself temporarily in another's shoes. Your boss will be trying to project his own personality into his speech, and the most you can do as his assistant is to aid that effort. So, if you draw such an assignment, don't be disappointed as long as your paragraphs are even faintly recognizable in the final product.

Prepare a Speech Release

I have already touched briefly on what you can do to get some advance publicity for your speech engagement.

A logical follow-up is to take along with you to the meeting a press release that the program chairman or other functionary can hand to the press. If it's an occasion when reporters from several publications are likely to show up, have enough copies to go around and leave one for the chairman or convention press agent to retain.

The release should be a short résumé of the speech, at the most not more than two double-spaced typewritten pages. At the top of page 1 place the line, "For release June 3,——P.M."—the approximate time the speech will be delivered. Its opening sentence may condense one of the most pungent thoughts in the speech and tie it to the speaker and the occasion. Here are examples of the opening sentences of two actual releases.

Washington, D.C., February 17—Keith Funston, president of the New York Stock Exchange, declared tonight that the demands of the space age will require an outpouring of capital that dwarfs anything the United States has attempted to raise previously.

He told the Association of Stock Exchange Firms here that the New York Stock Exchange estimates now put the corporate bill for new plants and equipment at an average of $45 billion a year between now and 1965. This compares with 1955 projections of about $35 billion a year.

St. Louis, Mo., February 25—Vast scientific illiteracy on the part of the public is dangerous because the public, not the scientists, will eventually determine how American science will progress, Gen. John E. Hull, president of the Manufacturing Chemists Association, said here tonight.

Gen. Hull, MCA president, spoke before members of the Chamber of Commerce of Metropolitan St. Louis.

Some organizations ask speakers for the full text of their speeches for possible publication and for their files. If you put your speech in manuscript form, make at least an original and two copies to supply this requirement. Keep one carbon for your own files, along with the material used in its preparation.

Summary

However you expect to deliver your speech, write it if you're anxious to make your best effort and to be explicit in what you say. This will also give you a copy of your work to use on future occasions.

A speech in manuscript differs from other types of writing:

1. It is broken into more clearly definable parts.

2. The style is more conversational and should include fewer statistics and elaborate allusions.

Think out fully what you want to say before writing anything but a few notes.

Your task is to put into your speech manuscript two essential qualities: clarity and color.

Clarity

1. Have you said anything that could be interpreted in more than one way?

2. Is it as simply and directly phrased as you can make it?

3. Do you get straight to the point?

4. Can it be strengthened by taking out any unnecessary adjectives and adverbs?

5. Are there words and technical terms that will be Greek to a considerable part of your audience?

6. Are the sentences short and to the point?

Color

1. Have you become so interested in tight reasoning toward conclusions that you've made dull reading out of it?

2. Are you making the most of your vocabulary, expressing your ideas in different and interesting ways?

3. Do you make intelligent use of words learned in general reading and of the many reference works available?

4. Can you improve your style by using more figures of speech?

If you write a speech for someone else to deliver, try to become an actor for the assignment. Think and write as you feel would show him at his very best.

Prepare a short press release containing several highlights, written in the newspaper style of descending importance.

CHAPTER 8

How to Set the Stage

A GOOD play and a good cast depend upon a stage manager to provide the physical setting and arrangements conducive to a good performance. In a limited sense, you must be your own stage manager.

Therefore it is important to arrive at the meeting place ahead of time and give it a last-minute inspection. Be sure that all your properties are in the right place and *in good working order*. Don't take charge of the affair; if any changes in arrangement are needed, suggest them to the chairman and let him see that they are made.

If you're speaking from notes or manuscript, a lectern is highly desirable if one is available. Check to see that it stands at the right height for you. Some table lecterns are too low for a fairly tall speaker when placed on the ordinary table, for instance. When that is the case, ask the chairman if he can obtain a box or other object to set it on and raise the lectern to a working eye level. Be sure, too, that there is light enough to read by.

If a microphone is to be used, see that it is set at the right height for you before you start speaking. By listening to previous speakers you can get a check on audibility. The business end of the mike should be tilted upward at about the level of your chin. Stand back or to one side so that your mouth is 10 to 12 inches from the mike. Try to avoid having the head of the mike obscure your face to part of the audience. Modern microphones are very sensitive. If you hear your voice coming back, you are too close.

Ideally, your mouth should remain the same distance from the mike at all times; otherwise the volume will be too strong at one time, too faint at another. Avoid speaking in a voice either too loud or too low. A very loud tone can cause a most annoying reverberation. If possible, have a scout in the back of the room with whom you've arranged a code to signal "Too low," "Too loud," or "OK."

A microphone restricts a speaker's freedom of movement to some degree. It takes an effort to adapt your gesturing to the device. Keep your arms free and don't handle the mike after you start speaking; that is a very distracting habit. If you're making a demonstration that requires walking about at some distance from the lectern, it will be necessary to have a portable microphone extension that you can hold in one hand.

The Personal Get-Ready

It's smart to eat lightly before speaking. A heavy meal is sedative. You wouldn't play tennis immediately after a large dinner. Public speaking demands physical effort, too. If you tax your stomach, your circulation will penalize your brain.

As for dress, a man should not wear a loud necktie or a sport shirt unless speaking at a barbecue where everyone else is similarly attired. If pictures are likely to be taken, or if he is appearing on television, he should wear a dark suit. Contrasts make good pictures, and a light suit with a white shirt has little contrast. A pale blue rather than a white shirt photographs better on television.

For women the right clothing is even more important than for men. Because of the greater choice available to women than to members of the drably dressed sex, women make more mistakes than men in dressing for a platform appearance.

Evelyn Mann of Houston, Texas, a prominent member of the International Toastmistress Clubs, has devoted considerable study to the subject of clothes for women speakers. In *The Toastmistress* magazine of June, 1961, she urges, "Plan ahead for coming occasions. Insure one basic dress appropriate to the season. Observe the dictates of quiet good taste."

Summoning up all my personal courage, I have discussed women's clothing with Mrs. Muriel Bryant, Vice-President, International Toastmistress Clubs. On the basis of her comments and my own observations of women on the platform, I offer the following suggestions.

You are more important than your clothes. They should not dominate you nor should they distract attention from you. Wear a simple dress with simple lines—preferably a dress of one color, two at the most. Eschew the severely tailored, or mannish style, and avoid elaborate frills. In fact, avoid all extremes of style.

Above all, don't wear clothes that require adjustment. You are on the platform to be heard, not to be examined. Don't wear tight clothes that will hike up when you gesture or when you stand up. Don't tug at your girdle or adjust shoulder straps. Don't wear a hat with a wide brim that conceals or casts shadows on your face.

Many women make the mistake of wearing too much jewelry when they speak in public. Your gems should be in your speech, not around your neck or dangling from your ears. Jewelry cannot be seen distinctly by the audience, but jewels can catch the light and sparkle distractingly.

If possible, wear a dress that has a pocket in which you can put your notes and your handkerchief. Carry a small purse but leave it at your seat when you approach the lectern. You won't need it while you are speaking, and it will be safe at your seat in full view of the audience.

While sitting and waiting your turn to speak, maintain an erect, but not rigid, posture. Don't sprawl. Keep your knees together and your dress pulled down. If you want to cross your legs, cross them at the ankles.

While this is not the place for such a complex subject as makeup, a few observations are in order. You are not about to undergo a screen test. Don't strive for exotic effects; go easy on rouge, eyebrow pencil, and eye shadow.

Strive for a natural effect. Select shades of makeup keyed to the color of your costume and flattering to your skin tones. And be sure to extend your makeup to your neck as well as your face.

Visual Aids Reinforce Your Words

There's an old principle of selling that says, "Tell them, and show them!" Since public speaking is primarily selling ideas to a crowd, it will pay in many instances to appeal to the eye with visual aids, as well as to the ear.

Not every speech, of course, is adaptable to visual aids. If your story is built around statistics to any degree, charts are suggested. It's hard to wring emotion out of figures, but you can give them appeal by visualizing them. When we get into the higher reaches, any statistic is interesting only in a relative way. To say that California's density of population is 100.4 persons per square mile of land area is just another figure, but to tell that this is more than Idaho, with 8.1, and less than Connecticut, with 517.5, gives your audience something to compare it with, removing it from an abstraction to a reality. The relative value of all statistics is further impressed when projected as a bar or pie chart.

There are six principal classes of visual aids adaptable to public speaking: (1) slide presentation; (2) flash cards; (3) flip charts; (4) recorded sounds; (5) movies; (6) chalk talk.

Slide Presentation

This should be regarded as a means of visualizing a speech and not as a program in itself. It should have an oral introduction and preferably a conclusion or summing up by the speaker. Unless you're unusually adept in doing two things at once, get an assistant to operate the projector. Use the cricket-sound device or a light signal to change slides, and thus avoid the "Next slide, please" interruption to your remarks. Don't repeat, "This slide shows. ..." Let the picture speak for itself, while you go on from there with your comment.

While we are accustomed to thinking only of color-film slides, all mounted in uniform size and projected onto a screen, the picture presentation idea is something bigger than this. By means of the opaque projector any photo, chart, or reading matter (whether printed, typewritten, longhand, or even a page of a book), in a wide range of sizes, can be projected on a screen and used to illustrate a talk.

Flash Cards

Such cards are prepared in advance and usually displayed on an easel. They consist of words, headlines, or charts that enable the speaker to fasten key ideas in his listeners' minds. Visuals of this sort should be short and simple enough to be grasped in five seconds, one idea to a card.

Flip Charts

These are drawn, usually in crayon or brush strokes, on a pad, typically of 100 sheets of paper, 24 by 36 inches in size. This is large enough to be seen easily by an audience of fifty or less. For larger audiences, larger sheets are needed. Unlike the flash cards, they are shown in fixed order by flipping each sheet over after it has been explained.

Recorded Sound

Pertinent sound effects may be synchronized with slides or used separately on records or tape. If amplifiers are needed, make sure the recorded sound is clear, understandable, and of adequate volume, yet not oppressively loud to normal ears.

Movies

Releases on nearly all subjects are available from corporations, trade associations, or public libraries. Investigate this possibility for supporting your speech. Or, you can take your own and show them yourself with a comparatively small investment. Remember, however, that films should always be regarded as visual aids, not speech substitutes.

Chalk Talk

This term covers any kind of lecture where the speaker does freehand drawing or lettering as he talks. It can be the most difficult of visual aids. If you attempt elaborate symbolical representations on a blackboard or easel pad you must carry these all in your head, since, when you turn to write or draw, you cannot have the benefit of notes. It must be done easily and spontaneously, and this comes only through laborious practice.

On the other hand, the use of a blackboard can be the simplest visual aid of all. This helps your listeners' memories. You may do nothing more than doodle with squares, triangles, and circles, each labeled to represent something. Action by the speaker in itself galvanizes attention.

An instructor of a class in salesmanship asked his students, "Now, what are some of the signs that a prospect is sold and it's time to try for a close?"

"When he asks about terms," a member of the class answered.

The instructor repeated the point, then wrote on the board, "Asks terms."

"And what else?"

He went on in the same way until he had five signs down on the board, all contributed by the class. Then he took up each one in order and discussed it, finally adding two points not suggested by students.

Observe These General Rules

Whether you use these or other visual methods, they will be more effective if you take certain precautions and follow established success rules.

1. In a fully visualized talk, visualize everything you talk about, and talk about every idea you visualize while it is being shown.

2. The visual point should be crystal clear, at least when supplemented by a few words of oral explanation.

3. Test to determine that your visuals can be seen by all your viewers.

4. Watch constantly that you don't get in the line of vision and obstruct the view of anything you're showing. If you're right-handed and are using a pointer, stand with the chart on your right, so that you won't be turning your back on the audience.

5. Talk *toward* your audience and keep facing your listeners as much as possible.

6. Give your projector or other mechanical gadgetry a last-minute check to see that it's working and the electric current is connected.

7. A room or hall doesn't have to be completely darkened for the proper showing of film or slides. There should be no stray light playing on the screen, but total darkness is not desirable because it precludes note taking or eye contact by the speaker.

Stage Properties and Demonstrations

The physical devices for dramatizing a discourse are limited only by the speaker's imagination.

Charles L. Lapp, Professor of Marketing at Washington University, has a speech that he calls "Six Steps to Sales Success." He sets up an ordinary stepladder on the rostrum and climbs it as he gets on with his six steps, until he comes to the climax, standing with one foot on the sixth rung of the ladder of success.

Part of Lapp's showmanship for this lecture is a succession of hats he uses for quick changes on the stage to illustrate several types of salesmen.

If your mind runs easily to demonstrations, they can be a most effective way to inform an audience or illustrate an abstract thought. But a warning is in order. Don't strain for an illustration, and never try to be a vaudeville artist when you're billed for a speech. When props become more than adjuncts to the spoken words, consider carefully before using them. The chief hazard is that the more intelligent members of an audience may believe the show is too elementary for them. Then there is the ever-present risk of a fumble that may cost you more than you gain.

The common habit of passing around pictures, printed matter, or samples before or during a speech can be a real liability. Hold them until after the meeting, and announce that those who wish may examine the material closely. During the speech, all attention should be focused on the rostrum, and diversions of any kind are to be avoided if possible.

A club committee had compiled and printed a rather ambitious history of the organization, and one committee member had been delegated to review the book in a thirty-minute speech. When he came to the meeting early and found that other members of the committee had set up a table near the entrance of the meeting room to distribute the history to members, he complained vociferously. "Put that book in their hands before the meeting and they'll be leafing through it all the time," he said. "I couldn't get their attention with a pistol. Don't distribute the books until after I speak." His advice was taken, and wisely.

In Conclusion

Before selecting any form of visual aid, you must decide the basic question. "Will it help me get my points across to my listeners?" Your speech is an effort to use sound to enter your listeners' minds through their ears. When you attempt to enter their minds through their eyes, your utilization of this additional sense must supplement and strengthen the appeal to their ears rather than compete with it. Use visual aids to clarify your points, to impress them on the memory, and to hold the interest of your listeners. Do not use visual aids if they will distract your listeners from what you are saying.

Summary

Nine pointers to remember in setting the stage for your speech.

1. Write your speech outline first; then look for visual aids that will illustrate what you want to say, rather than fit your speech to the visuals.
2. In any photography magazine you'll find advertised a wide choice of 16-millimeter color slides that are probably more professional than those you could take yourself. Some may suit your subject exactly, and the cost is not high. (Or your local photo shop can help.)
3. When displaying slides without sound, it isn't necessary to talk continuously. Let everything you say *supplement* the picture story. Talk to the viewers, not the screen or chart.
4. Keep your visuals and other props covered until you're ready to use them.
5. Be sure the visual aid or screen is high enough to be seen above the heads of viewers by those in the rear. Some rearrangement of the seating may be necessary to get everyone accommodated.
6. Set up everything you can before the meeting starts.
7. Use chalk that contrasts well with the blackboard, such as white on black or a light-colored chalk on a green board. The end should be blunt enough to make heavy lines.

8. In a group conference of fifteen or fewer, arrange the seats in a circle or around a table. If the conferees are spread out widely they're more likely to get into separate colloquies themselves.

9. Arrange in advance for any assistants you may need in the audience.

CHAPTER 9

How to Use Your Voice

THE ideal voice is clear, pleasant, expressive, with a ring of assurance and authority and a variety of intonation.

A story is told of an English actor who, as a dinner guest, was asked to recite something. He gave the Twenty-third Psalm, to applause from the company. Then he turned to a venerable clergyman who was present and asked if he would mind reciting the same passage. When the old man had finished, there was no applause, but an acknowledgment in bowed heads, while a few wiped tears from their eyes. The actor's comment was, "I reached only your eyes and ears, my friends, but this man reached your hearts. I know the Twenty-third Psalm: he knows the Shepherd." Both recited the same words. One put into them elocution, the other feeling.

Speakers often capitalize on a distinctive voice. In the South a voice with a Dixie trade-mark is an asset to a politician. Al Smith's East Side New York inflection made him beloved in his home city and remembered elsewhere. Joe Martin has a down-East inherited accent that he says "has been a distinct political asset in Massachusetts. The Scotch thought it was Scotch and the Irish thought it was Irish brogue, and I was content to have each think as he did and take me for his own."

Speakers like Floyd Gibbons and Walter Winchell made capital out of their ability to fire their sentences in machine-gun volleys.

Women have special problems in using their voice. The feminine voice is generally acknowledged to be more pleasing to the ear, but it lacks the timbre and resonance of the male voice. As a consequence, listeners often complain of a woman speaker that she runs her words together, or that she cannot be heard distinctly.

If you have this problem, practice speaking several notes below your normal tones. This will exercise and relax your vocal cords. It will also compel you to breathe deeper and put more force behind your words. Speak more slowly than is your custom, and use your lips more, pronouncing each word distinctly and precisely.

Use Your Voice to Hold Attention

Audience interest is killed by monotones. Give greater inflection to your sentences. Change your pace. Go slowly on your main points, to let them sink in. Then speed up as you pile on supporting evidence. Or, if you have been speaking rapidly and emphatically to drive home an idea, pause, lower your voice, and speak slowly as you state your conclusion.

Your voice is an instrument, powerful yet delicate, with infinite resources to help you. Like Haydn's *Surprise Symphony* with its sudden volumes of sound to awaken sleepers, your abruptly increased vocal volume will arrest attention as you emphasize a point. Conversely, a sudden drop in your voice suggests that you are taking the audience into your confidence.

The great preachers have learned above all others to avoid monotony as they would the seven-year itch. In his advice to fellow members of the cloth, the famous Charles H. Spurgeon said: "Keep on, on, on, on with commonplace matter and monotonous tone, and you are rocking the cradle, and deeper slumbers will result; give the cradle a jerk and sleep will flee."

Hold your audience interest by sounding like a human being: let your voice reflect your feelings. If you are angry or speak in protest or compassion or love or with amusement, you do not need to be told how to express these feelings with your voice. With most people, the voice is a natural vehicle for expressing their emotions. Something happens with beginners in front of an audience, however. Don't repress your feelings vocally, merely because you are addressing many people instead of another person. The emotion expressed in your voice may do more to awaken a response in your listeners than any ideas you may express. Emotions are contagious.

From your position, you can see the audience as a whole. When they are under your influence they will be very quiet, with only an occasional movement noticeable here and there. Most faces will be turned toward you, motionless. Coughs will be rare. If there is considerable movement, head turning, or coughing, your listeners are restless and you are losing them. You must take quick measures to meet the situation, chiefly by changes in your voice and manner of delivery.

The Voice Components

In order to understand how we can best utilize our vocal resources, it is necessary first to take stock of them and analyze what they are. Let's take a closer look at these general qualities: (1) volume; (2) pitch; (3) tone; (4) modulation and accent; (5) enunciation and pronunciation.

Volume

Voice volume is nothing more than loudness. It is a register of the force and energy with which sounds are emitted from the throat. The first thing to remember—and an astonishing number of amateurs, and some who regard themselves as professionals, forget it—is that in any kind of public address it is always necessary to speak louder than in natural conversation. The first mistake an amateur is likely to make is to talk too low. Always address yourself to the people in the back row.

Shouting, though, is something else again; it is to be avoided. In our time the worst offenders in this respect are exhorting evangelical clergymen and demagogic politicians. Their style seems to be predicated on the idea that a speaker's earnestness can be registered in decibels. Most listeners will agree with Dr. Ralph Smedley that "I do not like to be shouted at unless danger threatens."

Many clerical speakers place an undue reliance on vehemence of utterance. Of this fault, the Rev. George I. Myers, Protestant minister of Springfield, Missouri, says:

"Many young men considering the ministry seem to think their pulpit effectiveness is measured by a free style of delivery which includes shouting, gesticulating, and movement. They see this manner demonstrated by many speakers in commercial callings and are sometimes encouraged by members of their congregations who seek entertainment rather than spiritual commitment. The fact remains that the germ idea in a good thought should carry its own weight in the mind of an attentive listener and does not depend on vocal gymnastics or a 'sales gimmick.'"

A clergyman more than any other speaker is subject to a critical and unremitting surveillance by his congregation. Pulpit mannerisms—leaning on the pulpit, standing on tiptoes, taking off and putting on glasses repeatedly, and standing with hand in pocket—will be interpreted as lack of poise and dignity befitting the occasion of devotional services.

Pitch

Pitch is the frequency of vibrations in sound waves. We distinguish musical tones, like A and B, by their pitch, or "height in the scale." Actually, the human ear detects only a narrow range of all the sound that exists. For example, your dog can be called by a whistle pitched so high that you and I cannot hear it, although he can. At the other extreme, the pitch of a sound can be so low that it is indistinguishable by human ears.

A speaker's voice should range from about three notes below his natural pitch to about three above it. To discover your natural pitch, find on a piano the note that corresponds to your speaking tone.

A woman's voice has a higher pitch than a man's. A

man's vocal cords are normally half again as long as a woman's. This gives men a natural advantage over women in public speaking, although a woman who makes the most of her voice endowment can become an excellent speaker.

Under the stimulus of excitement and argumentation, speakers tend to pitch their voices too high because they become tense. Such a voice can easily range into the falsetto. It becomes harsh, querulous, unpleasant. A lower pitch carries the suggestion of poise and authority. To achieve this, relax your throat muscles, breathe more deeply than normal, and practice speaking in lower tones.

Tone

Tone can be defined as the quality of a voice. It is controlled by volume and pitch—and something else. This "something else" puts into the voice what we mean when we say that a person speaks in a conciliatory tone or a threatening tone, a kindly tone or a gruff tone, a commanding tone or a wheedling tone, a guarded tone or one of camaraderie. Here are the color and variety that go into the voice. If you have a dog that is devoted to you, you will have noted that it isn't the loudness with which you speak that causes him either to jump on you fondly or come as an abject culprit, tail between his legs and licking your hand by way of conciliation. There's something in your voice that tells him when you're friendly and when you're angry at him; it is not the loudness, the actual words, nor necessarily the pitch.

The average voice is said to have a range of seven or eight tones. In a speech you'll probably use half of this scale. The most common voices are known as normal, orotund, guttural, and whisper. The orotund gives your speech a flavor that goes with oratory: a sort of ringing lilt, fuller and more musical than normal. When exaggerated, it can easily sound bombastic and pompous; but used with restraint, it conveys the suggestion that what you're saying is important and that you believe it.

The guttural tone is throaty, coming from way down deep in the larynx. A man naturally uses it when he's in a gruff mood. A dog's growl or a bull's fighting bellow are guttural. But a man can employ the guttural tone artificially when it seems appropriate.

Speakers occasionally attain dramatic effects with the well-known stage whisper. It is said that Walter Hampden, the actor, could whisper in a way that could be heard and understood in the second balcony of a large theater.

Tone variation provides the color that makes a speaker's voice express feeling as well as thought. On the platform, put some resonance into your voice. Speak with authority.

Most inexperienced speakers sound uninteresting and dull because they speak in flat monotones. Fuller breathing and wider opening of the mouth help to take off this limitation.

If your chest moves up and down with every breath, you are breathing incorrectly. You should breathe from your diaphragm, and if you use this properly you will be able to feel it expand and contract.

An old-time voice teacher at a divinity school is remembered by one of his students for this epigram: "You can put your mind into your sermon, and you can put your heart into it; but until you can put your diaphragm into it, it won't amount to much."

Modulation and Accent

We use "modulation" here in the sense of manipulating volume, pitch, and tone to obtain desired effects. Your utterances need both highlights and shadows. You have been working up to a climax in drawing a word picture of some great wrong that cries out for righting. Now switch on the contrasting low modulation.

What I am saying amounts to this: A speaker's voice must not become a flat plain. Vary it by putting in some hills and mountains. A speech, as well as a piece of prose writing, should be punctuated.

Thomas E. Dewey is a speaker no one ever has trouble understanding. He enunciates with crystal clarity, never shouts, and always ends a declarative sentence on a downward inflection. Some speakers seek for an emotional rising inflection, but as a rule this is not good. In reciting a series of names or categories, many expert speakers do upbend on all except the last of the series.

On the other hand, there is a type of question that is asked with a downbend at the end: usually it is rhetorical and calls for a lengthy answer, says James H. Bender in his *How to Talk Well*. "We may well ask, from where is all this money to come?" "If this policy is to continue, how can we avoid positive calamity?" "Will my opponent please explain what he would do when this crisis arrives?"

After a speech has been written, the words and phrases to be emphasized should be fastened in the mind through drilling.

In the passages that follow, we have italicized the accented words. The first is from Dr. William Osler's lecture, "Teaching and Thinking."

"There are only *two* sorts of doctors; those who practice with their *brains* and those who practice with their *tongues.*"

The next example is from Abraham Lincoln's speech at Springfield, Illinois, July 17, 1858.

We are now far into the fifth year since a policy was initiated with the avowed *object* and confident *promise* of putting an *end* to *slavery agitation*. Under the operation of that policy that agitation has not only *not ceased*, but has constantly *augmented*. In *my* opinion it *will not* cease until a *crisis* shall have been reached and passed. "*A house divided against itself cannot stand.*" I believe this government cannot *endure* half *slave* and half *free*. I do *not* expect the Union to be dissolved—I do *not* expect the house to *fall*—but I *do* expect it will cease to be *divided*. It will become *all* one thing or *all* the other.

For special emphasis, speak the important word with greater volume and forcefulness. Of course you will vary your stress over a range of several notes, depending upon the values attached to words and phrases and sentences.

Authorities differ as to where the stress belongs in the expression "of the people, by the people, for the people." Commonly the inflection has been put on the prepositions, *of, by,* and *for.* But in recent years some authorities have insisted that *people* is the word to accent. It is a debatable question. What to accent is part of the speaker's own interpretation.

Enunciation and Pronunciation

Making yourself understood depends in no small degree upon articulating your syllables as clearly as possible. Open your mouth and let the vowels come forth. Don't smother your consonants or lose them at the ends of words. Watch to see that you're not hissing your sibilants:s-sh-c-ch-j-z-zh. Use your lips to shape your words precisely.

Don't let your sentences fade out at the end. Many speakers seem to lose interest and tire of their sentences as they go along. Often the close of a sentence or paragraph is its climax, deserving special emphasis and distinctness.

I heard a college professor of history make a speech with frequent references to "government." Invariably he slurred the word into "govermunt."

So many Americans have fallen into the habit of always rendering the "u" or the "ew" sound as "oo" that it has become acceptable, and a great majority now say "Noo York" when literally and traditionally it should be "Nieu York." No one, of course, would say "foo" for "few," and yet there is as much reason for this as the popular enunciation of "new."

But beyond this license, a clearly mispronounced word is a "rebuke to your raising." "Herth" for "hearth" (harth) is never correct. Don't say "for-*mid*-a-ble" for "*for*-mi-da-ble," "mu-ni-*cip*-al" for "mu-*nic*-i-pal," "su-per-*flu*-ous" for "su-*per*-flu-ous." Mispronunciations jar the ears of sophisticated listeners.

Ways to Improve Your Speaking Voice

The voice, like the mind, should be cultivated. A man's voice is not something like his freckles or his bowlegs or his sinusitis that he has to learn to live with and be contented. If you doubt that your voice can be changed for the better, talk to one of the correctional speech therapists who work with speech-handicapped children. It is amazing to learn how they have taken what seemed to be confirmed and hopeless stutterers and helped them to talk normally.

Perhaps you are saying, "I have a job that occupies my days, and I can't take professional voice culture. What can I do by myself to use my voice potential better?" Well, there's much that you can do. To begin with:

Identify Your Vocal Weaknesses

Find out just what you most need to correct. Make a recording of your rendition of a speech selection or of an original composition. Play back tape or platter, listening closely for faults that call for correction. Draw up and fill out a questionnaire like the one shown below. Get your wife and two or three discerning friends to answer the same questionnaire. Then compare their answers with your own. Play the recording again and try to evaluate the questionnaire answers. This should point up some of your speech habits that need correcting.

VOICE EVALUATION QUESTIONNAIRE

1. Did I talk too loudly? _____ Too softly? _____
   About the right volume? _____
2. Is my voice pitched too high? _____ Too low? _____
   About right? _____
3. Did I speak too fast? _____ Too slowly? _____
   About right? _____
4. Did I speed up or slow down toward the finish? _____
5. Did I enunciate clearly? _____
6. Did I slur over or mumble any syllables? _____
7. Was anything wrong with my pauses? _____
8. Did I mispronounce any words? _____

Practice Voice Exercises

Talking in front of a mirror is helpful for watching your breathing as well as posture and gestures. Practice uttering Dr. Wilfred Funk's "ten most beautiful English words": dawn, lullaby, tranquil, luminous, golden, hush, murmuring, mist, chimes, melody. Then you might try uttering some of the more vocally unpleasant or difficult words, such as cognate, consciousness, extraordinary, pachyderm, nebulous, particularize, recuperate, pharisaical.

For an extended course of exercises in controlled breathing and a full exposition of voice utilization and development, see Ralph C. Smedley's little book, *The Voice of the Speaker*, published by Toastmasters International, Santa Ana, California.

Read Aloud

This can be made a most agreeable diversion, while drilling yourself in both enunciation and pronunciation. Read aloud to one or more members of your family, consciously striving to apply the principles and practices recommended in this chapter. Time yourself occasionally, aiming at a speed of 125 to 150 words a minute. Speak in conversational tones. And *listen* to what you are saying so that the right words are emphasized. At the end of a sentence, pause long enough to breathe. You will observe that ease of utterance depends in part on the diction used. A speech can be so written as to be punctuated by natural pauses. Good examples will be found in the prose writings of Robert Louis Stevenson. Perhaps more than that of any other great English language writer, Stevenson's prose is easy to read aloud. Try his essay on "Talk and Talkers." Here are representative selections.

Literature in many of its branches is no other than the shadow of good talk; but the imitation falls far short of the original in life.... All sluggish and pacific pleasures are, to the same degree, solitary and selfish, and every durable bond between human beings is founded on or heightened by some element of competition.... Talk should proceed by instances; by the apposite, not the expository. It should keep close along the lines of humanity, near the bosoms and businesses of men, at the level where history, fiction and experience intersect and illuminate each other.

Read fiction aloud, particularly stories or novels that are liberally interspersed with dialogue. Ernest Hemingway was one of the great masters of dialogue in our time. In reading a story such as *The Killers* or a chapter from *For Whom the Bell Tolls,* practice speaking in a changed tone as one character succeds another in the dialogue.

Drama is excellent for this purpose. In Hamlet's speech to the players you combine the exercise with the bard's own instruction on how one should speak before a crowd.

If you can assemble even three or four persons for an evening, take several copies of a great play, assign the parts, and read them. Make it a game in which each participant tries to voice what he believes his character or characters actually feel.

Make the Most of Your Vocal Faculty

As you practice reading, it will be apparent that there is a right and a wrong way to use your voice. When huskiness or increasing hoarseness follows continued speaking, it is an indication that your vocal cords are not being used properly. Your voice is being forced. You can relax the throat muscles by bringing up your words from deeper down in the larynx. Project your voice all the way from your diaphragm. This provides the required volume, within your natural limitations, of course. In ordinary conversation you do not have to speak this way.

At its best, a speaker's voice is a magnificent instrument, adding to the effectiveness of a speech by assisting listeners to understand it, arousing their emotions, and holding their attention. Badly used, a monotonous, flat voice with poor enunciation will nullify a speaker's efforts to communicate because his listeners will stop listening. So, speak at a lower pitch, but with volume and distinctness. Speak slowly and with feeling. Your voice will then reflect the warmth and interest you want to instill in your listeners.

For Ladies Only

There was a period, before your time, when a woman who expected to do much public speaking would expose herself to instruction in "elocution." The horrible result was usually twofold. Every vowel was spoken with its written value (she would say "ac-tor" instead of "act'r"), and her range of inflection was forced into a studied pattern of excessive highs and lows that sounded like singing a tuneless operatic aria. The style has nearly died out; but, strangely enough, some women today, though untrained, are mesmerized into similar errors when they find themselves on the platform.

Reviewing our five voice components, here is a check list adapted specially for the woman before an audience.

1. Volume: as high as you can hold it comfortably.
2. Pitch: as low as you can hold it comfortably.
3. Tone: practice richness and roundness; avoid shrillness.
4. Modulation: moderate in range; at least cut off high peaks.
5. Pronunciation: correct but conversational.

Summary

Your voice and manner of delivery can be a prime asset in holding your audience's attention. A good public speaking voice should be clear, agreeable, varied, and expressive.

These qualities are obtained through three controls: volume, pitch, and tone. Their manipulation is by means of modulation and accent. Words, phrases, and sentences are varied in intensity and tone in order to relieve monotony and put feeling and values into what the speaker is saying.

Full enunciation of syllables is far more necessary in public speaking than in conversation. Correct pronunciation is taken for granted as a mark of education and refinement.

Voice can be improved by critical evaluation from recordings and by persistent practice in speaking at your best.

To avoid strain on the vocal cords from prolonged use, draw up your words from deep down in the throat and diaphragm, opening your mouth to let them escape unhindered.

CHAPTER 10

How to Influence Opinion

IF YOU learn that you can influence the opinion of others through your talks, your ability to do so may have a profound effect on your own life. If you couple this gift with idealism about one or more issues or goals, you may find that many of your speeches will be for the purpose of influencing opinion. Politically, you may campaign for candidates or issues on the local, state, or national level; you may wish to guide public thought on issues of more immediate concern to your audience, such as school bonds or taxes. You may be a salesman whose livelihood depends upon persuading prospects to buy your products.

Within your business firm, your success depends constantly on making a positive impression; the ability to express your ideas matters greatly there. In your club, your church—wherever you are working or playing with your associates—there will be differences of opinion and decisions to be made. Your ability to change the attitude of others and to affect their judgment will shape your success, your achievement of leadership, and, to a great extent, your future. Therefore, whatever the circumstances, your knowledge and skill in the art of molding opinion is the most important and useful form of public speaking you can master.

There are three prerequisites to your success in influencing the opinion of others.

1. You must care about the issue and the audience.
2. You must believe that your talks can be effective.
3. You must know what you want from your audience, and you must consider realistically whether your purpose can be achieved.

You Must Care about the Issue and the Audience

Emphasis is on "you." Influence, like charity, begins at home. If *you* don't really care, your audience will know it. And if you don't care, *they* won't care. This is just another way of saying that you must be sincere and earnest. Sincerity and earnestness are intangible, but they are indispensable to the speaker who would influence the opinions of others.

You Must Believe that Your Talks Can Be Effective

Many political speeches do not actually influence the opinions of listeners concerning specific issues; they merely put the speaker's views on record. These speeches do not attempt to change opinion. They aim to enlist the support of those who already hold the same opinion as that of the speaker, so that he may be elected, or so that he may have the backing necessary to act on behalf of the opinions expressed. To influence opinion, therefore, may not mean to change it, but to reinforce it, to strengthen it, to articulate it for others, to influence others *not* to change their views. President Lyndon B. Johnson, adapting a thought from Bismarck, has said that politics is the "art of the possible." So is the public speaking that influences opinion.

Any successful salesman will tell you that his most effective assets are his belief in his product, his genuine conviction that he is benefiting customers by selling to them, and his confidence in his ability to influence them, now. Without these essentials, your speeches will be like those of Leosthenes, of whom Plutarch said, "His speeches are like cypress trees. They are tall and comely, but bear no fruit."

You Must Know What You Want from Your Audience

We have been considering your belief in yourself, in your point of view, in your ability to influence the opinions of your listeners. These are subjective elements. You must also be realistic if you are to succeed in talking to influence opinion. You must know what is possible and decide what you want from your listeners. If you want your audience to do something, to think or feel something *now*, you will use one kind of approach; if you are after long-range results, if you wish to alter opinion on a matter that will remain an issue for years, you will use another.

Suppose you argue in favor of vivisection before a

meeting of the Anti-vivisection Society. If you attempt to persuade your listeners to agree with your opinion that vivisection under humane conditions is a boon to mankind, you will probably win few immediate converts, but you may plant ideas that stimulate a new line of thought among many listeners. Perhaps a year or two hence, they will change their positions—but not today.

Analyze your purpose in speaking and what you want from your audience. If you are speaking in court, or as a member of a jury, or as a member of a committee, or to a club that has a motion on the floor, you are talking to a group already committed to take action. The only question is, *which* action. In any situation involving a fairly definite time of decision and a choice of specific alternatives, you have a reasonably good chance of influencing opinion.

Organization of Speech to Influence Opinion Now

There are many ways to organize such a speech, some of which were touched on in Chapter 6, but the simplest and one of the most effective is this:

1. State the problem or the condition.
2. Identify its causes.
3. Define the issue or the action needed.
4. Propose your solution.
5. Show how your proposal will eliminate the causes, alleviate the effects, or otherwise solve the problem satisfactorily.
6. Show that your proposal is the only practical or effective solution or better than any other.
7. Tell the audience what you want them to do to put your idea to work.

Long-Range Influence on Opinion

If you are planning to make a speech on civil rights or some similar religious or moral issue, you should recognize that deep-rooted opinions on such subjects are rarely if ever changed in one day or by one speech. If public opinion were that erratic, we should indeed be living in an unstable world. Yet, opinion does change and can be influenced, even in these areas.

Speeches like yours do carry weight. Attitudes and opinions are always in the process of change, and this is guided gradually by many speakers over a period of time. None of us thinks today about education, income taxes, popular elections, slavery, art, or literature as our parents or grandparents thought—or, perhaps, even as we ourselves thought a few years back. Others have influenced our thinking by degrees and from day to day, although it cannot be said of anyone that at two o'clock this afternoon he is going to reverse his opinion on labor unions in general or on the National Association of Manufacturers.

Four Practices for Influencing Opinion

The knowledge of how to influence opinion is not new, and it has never been a secret. The principles were known to Aristotle, Cicero, Quintilian, Demosthenes, Mark Antony, and Jesus Christ, to cite only a few. In the last fifty years our understanding of the principles of persuasion and the details of their application has been improved. The soundness of anciently established principles has been confirmed by anthropologists, psychologists, sociologists, political scientists, advertisers, and students of public speaking. Public speaking to influence opinion is still an art, but science has contributed to its effectiveness.

As with any art, no one can spell out rules guaranteed to make the practitioner an artist. However, there are four major practices that, if applied, will enhance your ability to influence opinion, on either short-range or long-range issues.

1. You must get the audience to accept you, taking into account their prevailing attitudes and prejudices.

2. You must base your reasoning and evidence on deep-seated wants and culture patterns.

3. You must use indirect as well as direct methods.

4. You must tell your listeners what you want them to think, feel, or do.

Get the Audience to Accept You

The emphasis once more is on *you*. If a man likes *you*, trusts *you*, finds something about *you* that inspires his confidence, both consciously and unconsciously, he is more inclined to accept what you say. In fact, he may not even be aware of it, but if he likes and admires you he *wants* to think like you. This psychological process is called "identification."

In your own experience, I'm sure you have said to yourself, as you listened to one speaker, "I wouldn't believe him if he swore on a stack of Bibles," and of another, "He talks my language" or "He's my kind of person." That's identification.

*Five Ways to Establish Identification with
Your Listeners*

Your listeners may identify with you, or they may identify you with themselves or with something they find admirable. There are recognized methods of encouraging the identification process.

1. *Indicate personal association.* If the facts permit, find an opportunity to identify specifically with a remark such as "I was born and grew up here, and I'm one of you." Or, "I, too, am a lawyer" or realtor or whatever the listeners in your homogeneous audience may be. But if you have to stretch to find a remote and general link in your personal life that you share with your audience, be careful. It may be better to use some other method of identification. If you say vaguely to high-school or college students, "I, too, was once a student," or "I was young once myself," they have probably heard these platitudes so often from those who followed the remark with reprimands or advice that they will identify you with people who have lectured them rather than with themselves.

2. *Identify with your listeners' beliefs, desires, or welfare.* You utilize this kind of identification when you say, directly or in effect, "Like you, I want our city to grow," or "I, too, believe in better schools," or "We all want peace."

3. *Identify with generally accepted or approved ideals, values, and principles.* Religion, community spirit, service to others, are common denominators and unifying bonds on which many organizations are built. If you are talking to a luncheon meeting of a service club such as Lions, Kiwanis, or Sertoma, you know that its members are actively concerned with community service projects, and if you belong to a similar association, then you and your listeners "speak the same language." Most groups have similar and predictable feelings about property, family security, freedom, recognition, and fair play, to name only

a few. If you and your listeners want the same thing, you have something important in common. You see things as they do. You are like them. You are to be trusted. Your ideas are to be accepted.

But don't be banal or condescending or too obvious. Your audience will resent you if you indicate that you *expect* to be accepted just because you have some views in common or belong to the same church.

4. *Avoid unfavorable identification, if possible.* To do this, you must know the prevailing attitudes of your listeners. You would obviously express an argument for civil rights differently in New York than in Mississippi.

When a controversial point of view is not germane to your argument, try to avoid it. For instance, if you are talking about the values of higher education, do not bring in the fact that you are a Democrat or a Republican, in the hope that most of your audience will accept you or your views on education for that reason. If your subject is economic development in the South and your audience is in Birmingham, Alabama, it is not helpful or pertinent to refer to your life membership in the NAACP or the American Civil Liberties Union. You are not being deceptive or dishonest; you are merely not mentioning differences that have little to do with your subject and would alienate your listeners unnecessarily.

5. *Identify yourself with your listeners by being the kind of person they feel they can trust.* You cannot say, "Believe me because I'm a gentleman; I'm honest; I am trustworthy and reliable." When the part was overplayed in *Hamlet,* the Queen said, "The lady doth protest too much, methinks."

You communicate with your listeners by a great variety

of methods. Your dress, your pronunciation, your choice of language, your courtesy and general manner—all give your audience a basis for judging you. And they will. How you present your material will tell your audience about you. Do you make broad assertions? Are you given to exaggerations? Do you use statistics and facts accurately and draw reasonable, conservative conclusions from them? Are you obviously forcing or feigning enthusiasm?

If you act and talk like a gentleman whose ideas are entitled to consideration, your audience will recognize the fact. If you sound like a sideshow barker, your audience will not buy your ideas.

There are five cardinal points to bear in mind if you want to avoid being unfavorably typecast by your listeners.

(*a*) Don't parade your prejudices.

(*b*) Don't name-call. Rest your case on facts or reason.

(*c*) Don't use propaganda for facts. Use reliable facts fairly.

(*d*) Don't pretend to be an expert if you're not. Quote experts.

(*e*) Don't claim too much or try to prove too much in one speech. But nail down what you assert.

Base Your Reasoning and Evidence on
Deep-seated Wants and Culture Patterns

To influence opinion, you must relate your point of view to the wants, the hopes, the needs, the ambitions, and the fears of others. All listeners have these. What the effective speaker does is to play upon them, like the harpist plucking the strings to produce the sound of harmony between listener and speaker. If you would influence your listeners' opinions, you must show how your proposal, your point of view, the action you want from your listeners, will satisfy their deep-seated wants.

It is apparently a favorite pastime of social scientists to classify and name the basic wants. From my own experience, I have developed the following list. You will probably wish to amend it according to your own knowledge of life and people.

1. People have basic physical hungers, such as food, sex, the need for warmth and physical comfort.

2. People want safety, for themselves and others. This includes financial security as well as physical safety; indeed, any factor contributing to self-preservation.

3. People want love. They want friendship and affection, and they want to feel needed—important to others.

4. People want individuality; they want to be themselves, not like any other person in the world. But not too different, either. Here we get into culture patterns. People want to be like those among whom they live, who do the same kind of work, and who are in about the same income range. They want to have self-respect; they want to have pride in themselves; they want social status.

5. People want self-fulfillment; they want to realize their potential as human beings. They seek to express themselves in music, in the arts, in every phase of human endeavor. People want to do better, to be better.

Of course, only social scientists can identify and classify human wants with such deceptive ease. Men are usually motivated by combinations of wants, and sometimes these are in conflict with one another.

The point is that you must draw upon your understanding of your audience's main drives if you would influence their opinions. If you are making a speech to the PTA on behalf of an additional tax levy for your city library, you will rely on your listeners' desire to help their children to a greater enjoyment of life and better preparation for success through a knowledge of good books. You will probably also appeal to their desire for self-fulfillment. To a group of businessmen, you would attempt to show that a library is related to their prosperity. It is a source of information helpful to them; it will attract the kind of residents who will be assets to the community; and so forth.

Use Indirect as Well as Direct Methods

The direct method is to meet an issue head on, to tell people they should change their opinions. Often this is not so successful as an indirect approach. "A man convinced against his will is of the same opinion still."

Professor James Harvey Robinson has written:

We are incredibly heedless in the formation of our beliefs, but find ourselves filled with an illicit passion for them when anyone proposes to rob us of their companionship. It is obviously not the ideas themselves that are dear to us, but our self-esteem, which is threatened. We are by nature stubbornly pledged to defend our own from attack, whether it be our person, our family, our property, or our opinion.... We may surrender, but rarely confess ourselves vanquished. In the intellectual world at least, peace is without victory.

Few of us take the pains to study the origin of our cherished convictions, indeed, we have a natural repugnance to so doing. We like to continue to believe what we have been accustomed to accept as true, and the resentment aroused when doubt is cast upon any of our assumptions leads us to seek every manner of excuse for clinging to them. The result is that most of our so-called reasoning consists in finding arguments for going on believing as we already do.

The reluctance of listeners to give up their opinions is the major reason for using indirect methods of influencing them. If a listener does not like your viewpoint, mentally he carries on a running argument with you, or, as you start, he says to himself, "I'm not going to listen to that fellow. There are a lot of answers to his arguments, even if I have to think of them later."

If you propose to persuade your listeners to change their points of view, one of your most effective methods will be indirection. Instead of expounding the merits of a program for a government-sponsored plan for medical care for the aged, you point out that the average life span of Americans is increasing, that there are more and more people living to a greater age than ever before, and older people are increasingly subject to infirmities, illness, and injury. They can be a severe financial burden on those who love them. Perhaps your listeners are concerned with their elderly parents. You tell the story of Jim and Mary, an average middle-income couple. Mary's mother fell and broke her hip. You recite all the costly financial, emotional, and domestic consequences of the mishap. Mary's parents were not charity cases, but their small pension and Social Security income was quite inadequate to meet hospital and doctor's costs. Neither did their hospital insurance come near covering the medical costs, and so forth. Under the proposed medical care program, of course, things would have been quite different.

The listener's prejudices are not aroused by the indirect

method, and controversy over specific proposals can often be side-stepped. Indirection is more suitable when you want to stimulate the desire of listeners to alter their opinions, which, as you well know, are governed by sympathies rather than by an evaluation of specific merits of your viewpoint. The direct method is more appropriate when you want to justify a change of opinion on the part of listeners who are inclined to analyze and weigh the relative merits of their opinions as compared with yours.

Tell Your Audience What You Want Them to Think, Feel, or Do

What you ask of listeners must be within the range of their performance. Recently I heard an eloquent speaker deliver an impassioned plea to a ladies' luncheon club to "Defend the Constitution!" The listeners were obviously moved and were ready to do whatever was asked of them, including, I am sure, physical assault on anyone who threatened the Constitution. But the ladies were frustrated. The speaker asked them to do something vague and general, but he didn't tell them what he expected of them or how they were to translate their feelings into actions. Within fifteen minutes after he finished, the speaker had lost his influence. The reaction of the ladies was summed up by a comment I heard at my table: "It was a wonderful speech, but so what?"

Don't be inconclusive. If you want a point of view to prevail or wish a decision or an action from your listeners, make this clear to them. The speaker who effectively exercises influence on the opinions of others is the one who gets their emotional and intellectual motors running and then tells the drivers how to shift into gear, giving direction and movement and a goal as an outlet for the generated energy.

Of course, as I have indicated earlier in this chapter, what you ask of your audience must relate to the situation or the issue on which you seek to influence them. Do you want a decision now? Is your audience already committed to act but undecided as to which action to take? What can this particular group reasonably be asked to do? Do you want them to vote, to write their congressmen? To act in some way, or to alter their point of view? And be sure *you* know what your listeners should do. Don't ask them to protest to the city engineer if you have tried to influence their opinion on a matter pending before the city council.

If you want something specific from your listeners, be specific in telling them what it is. The other night I heard a speaker make his audience squirm over their civic apathy. But he didn't then follow through by showing them how to express their views in some meaningful action. He didn't influence his listeners; he merely scolded them.

There is an important exception to this point. If you are concerned with the opinions of your listeners on a profound moral or religious issue or one on which no immediate action or decision is called for, you do not need to be specific. In fact, it may be better not to ask anything definite of your listeners. All you want them to do as a result of the influence of your speech is that most difficult thing of all: to think. This is the obligation and the reward of the effective public speaker and the key to his ability to influence others.

Summary

There are three prerequisites for influencing opinion successfully: you must sincerely care about the issue; you must believe in your ability to convince your audience; and you must consider whether your purpose can best be achieved by striving for an immediate or long-range effect.

Once you have fulfilled these three needs, there are four practices that will help you prepare an effective speech.

1. You must get the audience to accept you, and to do this you will have to take into account their prevailing attitudes and prejudices. Some of the best ways of establishing identification are to (*a*) indicate personal association, (*b*) identify with the audience's beliefs, desires, or welfare, (*c*) identify with generally accepted ideals, values, and principles, (*d*) avoid unfavorable identifications, (*e*) establish an image of someone who can be trusted.

2. You must base your reasoning on deep-seated wants. Among these are the basic physical wants, a desire for safety and security, a need for love, and a striving for individuality and self-fulfillment.

3. You must use indirect as well as direct methods.

4. You must tell your listeners what you want them to think or do.

CHAPTER 11

How to Handle the Question Period

IF YOU wish to invite questions and comments from the floor at the end of your speech, always ask your chairman whether this would be all right. If so, find out the approximate amount of discussion time available.

A question period is one of the speaker's rewards for having given an effective talk. Listeners may wish to know more about the subject, or they may want to contest some points. In any event, they have been aroused to interest and provoked to thought. You, as the speaker, have an opportunity on an informal basis to fill in gaps, emphasize topics, clarify misunderstandings.

However, you must know when *not* to solicit questions. A strictly inspirational talk, for example, usually should not be followed by a question period. It would serve only as an anticlimax, an emotional letdown. Under some circumstances (which you must judge for yourself), a political speech or one on a controversial subject may provoke questions or impromptu remarks from the floor that may mar the effect of your speech.

If There Are No Questions

A very embarrassing moment occurs if the chairman invites questions and the audience responds with silence. Sometimes this is just because no one wants to be first. This contingency can be avoided if you arrange with the chairman ahead of time to plant a question or two in the audience to get things started.

Another solution I have seen used effectively—especially with women's clubs, service clubs, and trade association groups—is for the speaker to say. "Well, if nobody has questions to ask *me*, then I have one or two I'd like to ask *you*." Then be sure your question is designed to reflect a genuine interest in your listeners and what they think; you must not sound like a schoolteacher testing whether the audience has really been paying attention.

Some people hesitate to ask a question because of fear of exposing their own ignorance. If you have an anecdote you can tell at your own expense (one that shows you are human and will not bite the questioner, or a story about an amusing question asked of you on some previous occasion), this may establish a warm, informal rapport with your listeners and start the ball rolling.

Set Up a Limitation

Do not hesitate to limit the area of your competence to answer questions. This will add authority to the answers you do present. Otherwise you may be drawn into the position of answering any and all questions thrown at you. If you are speaking to a group of specialists, you risk overextending yourself. Let's imagine you are addressing a convention of petroleum men on better human relations in industry. You do not know the oil business, and it is too much to expect you to apply your principles of personnel management specifically to that type of activity. Questions that begin, "That's all very well, Mr. Speaker, but what would you do in this situation that happened in one of our refineries?" are not fair. You can offer principles and methods that have worked in industry generally, but you are not competent to apply them to the intricate problems of a particular field. That's up to your listeners.

Guides for Answering Questions

1. *Don't answer unless you know the answer.* Your listeners will respect you more if you say candidly, "I don't know," than if you are evasive or vague or pretend to knowledge you do not possess.
2. *Answer briefly.* Some questions may tempt you to make a speech in reply. Don't do it. If the question is pertinent to the subject on which you have already spoken, answer it briefly. You had one chance to cover the answer in your speech, and whatever your reason for not doing so, a second speech will not increase the effectiveness of your first one. If the tempting question is not pertinent,

you should not answer it at all in most cases, and certainly you should not launch into an impromptu oration. Keep your answers brief but adequate, so that as many listeners as wish may participate in the question period.

3. *Recognize questions in order.* When two or more persons hold up their hands or rise at the same time, recognize the first one you see, then mentally note and come back to others next in order. Let your eyes roam over the entire room, including the head table or rostrum, if there is one. Embarrassment is created when listeners try again and again to get recognition for a question, but because they are not in the speaker's direct line of vision, they are ignored, usually in favor of more aggressive persons who may seek the spotlight of attention.

Try to give recognition to each person who has a question before giving any one of them a second opportunity. Your conduct of the question period can help your speech by confirming the impression that you are a fair person. Don't hesitate to hold off aggressive hand wavers by saying, "Will you hold it a moment, please? I believe this gentleman over on my far right is next." Then point to the person you want to recognize and ask for his question.

4. *Always repeat a question before answering it.* The entire group probably did not hear it. Often a question, as stated, may not be expressed with clarity. You are at liberty to restate the question, but make it clear that you are attempting to help both questioner and audience. You may also be helping yourself by snatching time to think about your answer. Do not hesitate to say, "As I understand it, you are asking..."

If you solicit written questions and expect many listeners to respond, it is usually desirable to have the chairman or someone else receive the questions and read them before passing them along to you. He can eliminate the questions in unreadable handwriting and the queries of cranks. In case you do not have assistance, at least play safe by reading the question to yourself before reading it to the audience.

5. *Avoid conversations.* Although questions and answers involve only two speakers, the exchange is, or ought to be, for the benefit of the entire audience. Do not be drawn into an extended exchange or conversation with one questioner. The audience may feel excluded and will lose interest. More likely, the questioner will not be clearly heard, so your answers will not mean much to the group as a whole.

6. *Always be courteous.* During the question period almost anything can happen. Most questioners seek information or clarification and deserve your patience and courtesy. Others may be critical, expressing doubt about an assertion or conclusion you have stated. You may be firm or emphatic, but you must maintain your courtesy if you would not forfeit the good will of your listeners.

You may be confronted by a heckler or someone who is thoroughly out of sympathy with your position and whose question is obviously stated to embarrass you. It is particularly effective, and important to you, that you maintain *your* courtesy. Audiences appreciate fair play and respond to good manners. If you refuse to be baited into a reply in kind, you have won an edge over your questioner.

This does not mean that you must always turn the other cheek. If necessary, you can be curt and still be courteous. Or, if you are sure of yourself, you can turn the tables with a humorous remark, as was done by a city man addressing an audience of farmers. One critical listener, seeking to expose the speaker's ignorance of agriculture, asked, "Hey, how do you tell a bad egg?" The speaker replied, "Well, if I had anything to tell a bad egg, I'd break it gently." That effectively quieted the adversary.

One way to handle an unfriendly questioner is to ask: "You seem to be in fundamental disagreement with what I've been saying. Why don't you give us your own views in a few words?" If he accepts the invitation and proves to be a crackpot, he will quickly expose himself to the audience. Or he may make a vulnerable statement that you can readily refute. In any event, his impromptu speech will be compared with your prepared and rehearsed talk.

Under especially provocative circumstances a speaker is justified in making the kind of reply that General Hugh Johnson occasionally used: "I'll answer any fair question," he would say, "but I won't answer a loaded question like this one."

Two Factors Affect Audience Reactions

The basic purpose of questions and answers is the same as the purpose of a speech: to reach the minds of the audience. Therefore you must be sensitive to the psychological aspects of the question-and-answer situation that can affect the audience reactions to the questioner and to you.

Usually the audience is for the underdog. He speaks from their midst; he is, at least superficially, one of them. He, like them, is an unknown. He may be voicing their own doubts or reservations. He is physically handicapped, in the sense that he speaks from the floor, which is not a commanding position, and he probably does not speak into a microphone. He speaks impromptu. He is brave in speaking up, and secretly the crowd envies him. He is an amateur confronting a professional. Therefore, do not be discourteous or take undue advantage of your situation to subdue the one who has the sympathy of the audience. You will alienate them.

On the other hand, your advantages over questioners should make it possible for you to cope with any situation. Your advantages are many; some are obvious, some subtle. Let them work for you, but do not abuse them like a bully and thus push your listeners onto the side of the questioner by making them conscious of his underdog role.

He who possesses authority, power, and the advantage over an opponent and who exercises his assets with restraint and consideration wins admiration and appreciation. You have a "name," a reputation, knowledge of your subject. You have received top billing and have been given a good send-off by the chairman. You have at least the implied support or endorsement of the organization that asked you to speak. You have prepared your talk. You have some skill or experience in speaking. You have had the first crack at the audience and a longer exposure than your questioner. You have had a better opportunity to sell yourself and your point of view. You have the commanding position of the platform, and you have the public address system working for you. You stand alone, recognized and emphasized and usually several feet above the audience. You are in the position of leadership. Just as there is a latent or unconscious relationship between the listeners and the underdog questioner, so is there also an identification and a desire to be related with the leader:

you, the speaker. Cultivate this empathy; do not alienate it.

How to End the Question Period

Question periods often end in an atmosphere of uncertainty that concludes your performance on an anticlimactic note. The chairman may be inexperienced and doubtful whether to cut in and end the questions, so he hovers behind you or stands to one side, ostentatiously glancing at his watch, incidentally drawing attention away from you and stimulating the anticipatory rustling of the audience. Listeners begin to gather purses, gloves, and overcoats and ready themselves for departure.

Before opening the question period, confer briefly with the chairman. Agree on the length of the question period and who is to end it. When time is not a deciding factor, most chairmen are reluctant to break off a session as long as the audience is sufficiently interested to ask questions. If you want to stop, even though you agreed to leave this up to the chairman, do not be afraid to call a halt.

Don't let the session drag. If you have to solicit questions or hunt for waving hands, it is time to quit. Watch your audience for signs of restlessness, and wind up while the atmosphere is still lively and the audience interested. Let your listeners be in the comparable position of the wise diner who has enjoyed a good meal and pushes away from the feast wanting just a little bit more.

Sometimes you may find it graceful and convenient, when the pace of the discussion period has slackened, to offer to answer further questions after the meeting and then abdicate to the chairman. Thus you release the general audience but leave the door open for limited conversation with a few.

In any case, conclude the session with a brief expression of your appreciation of the questions, thank the audience or compliment them appropriately, and return the meeting to the chairman. It is sufficient if you step back from the lectern and say, "Thank you," or "The meeting is yours, Mr. Chairman." Do not announce, "I am now turning over the meeting to the chairman." This is neither accurate nor good form.

Summary

A good talk will often elicit questions from the floor, although on some occasions, such as after an inspirational or very controversial speech, it is better not to have a question period.

If you do desire a question period, it is usually a good idea to plant a speaker or two in the audience to start the ball rolling or even to put a question of your own to your listeners.

When answering questions, there are six points that should be kept in mind: (1) answer only if you are sure of your information; (2) answer briefly; (3) recognize questions in order; (4) repeat questions before answering; (5) avoid conversations; (6) always be courteous.

The length of the question period should be determined by the amount of time allotted the speaker or signs of audience restlessness, or both.

CHAPTER 12

How to Preside at a Meeting

PRESIDING at a meeting is a form of public speaking. However, the ability to give an effective speech is not enough to make you a good presiding officer.

In this age of committees, it is almost inevitable that sooner or later you will find yourself presiding over a group, whether it be a business, civic, or club committee, a panel, symposium, or conference, or a large and more formally conducted public meeting.

As a public speaker, you have one main purpose: to get your message across to your audience. But as a presiding officer, you must be able to direct the audience's attention to others. To guide and control the meeting, you must be able to speak publicly and authoritatively without making a speech.

Four Roles of the Presiding Officer

In 1939, Dr. Ralph C. Smedley, the founder of Toastmasters International, wrote a booklet entitled *The Amateur Chairman,* which has become one of the unsung best sellers in the publishing field. It has exerted an immeasurable influence on the conduct of presiding officers throughout North America. Now in its eleventh edition, it has sold nearly three quarters of a million copies. In it Dr. Smedley describes these four roles of the presiding officer:
1. To serve as a Pilot
2. To serve as a Referee
3. To serve as a Toastmaster
4. To serve as a Pinch Hitter

We shall consider each of these briefly, with enough attention to enable you to serve effectively as a presiding officer.

To Serve as a Pilot

You must know the purpose of the meeting, be able to control and guide it to its destination, and know when and how to stop it. Dr. Smedley observes: "One of the guaranteed ways of killing a meeting is to let it drag along without intelligent direction until the audience is tired out."

The Order of Business

Your navigation chart is the Order of Business. You must plan the meeting, or you doom it to failure. The

basic details of a meeting are covered in this generally accepted order:
1. Call to order
2. Announcements and introductions
3. Reading and approval of minutes of previous meetings
4. Reports of officers and standing committees
5. Reports of special committees
6. Unfinished business
7. New business
8. Program
9. Adjournment

This is standard operating procedure, but it is flexible. Variation or embellishment will not invalidate the meeting but may tangle its path. Invocation, pledge of allegiance, music, and other features may be inserted at appropriate points. As presiding officer, be sure to announce clearly each order of business as you come to it. Do not permit the introduction of any irrelevant subject.

As presiding officer, write out the Order of Business, including all the announcements and introductions you can anticipate, and check off each item as you guide the meeting past that point.

1. *Call to order.* There are many ways of calling a meeting to order. You may tap a spoon against a glass, bang your gavel, or blow a whistle, if necessary. If the group is large and unruly and music is available, play the National Anthem. The purpose of calling the meeting to order is to get attention and start the meeting. When you have quiet, say "The meeting will please come to order."

2. *Announcements and introductions.* If you have been

requested to make announcements, write them or ask for them in writing, so that you can state their contents completely, accurately, briefly, and slowly enough for the audience to note the details. If you intend to introduce guests or visitors, be sure that none are overlooked. Ask each to stand for a brief moment after your introduction. If you are going to introduce several, you may ask the meeting to withhold its applause until all have been introduced. Although some people enjoy the limelight, it is usually undesirable to ask guests to remain standing until all have been introduced. They don't know what to do with themselves during the other introductions; they may even wave to friends, talk, or distract attention. If you do not have the name of every guest, ask each member of the group who brought a guest or is seated next to one to rise and introduce the guest, *briefly*. Your own introductions also should be brief. Their purpose is to focus attention on the guest and to identify him, not extol him.

3. *Program.* In most well-conducted organizations a minimum of business is handled in open meetings (*i.e.*, meetings of the entire membership at which there may be non-member guests attending). Deliberations are made by the governing board, although some actions may have to be confirmed in open assembly. If business is to be taken up that is expected to require considerable discussion, it should be scheduled after the main program is over. Nothing will ruin a program more surely than dull, lengthy reports or prolonged discussions that do not permit the program features to get under way until the hour is late and the audience is bored or irritated.

In making an introduction, keep it short. Remember

that when you introduce a speaker you are graciously welcoming him and presenting him to the audience, and you have only to answer three basic questions:

(*a*) What is the speaker going to talk about?

(*b*) Why is he talking about this subject?

(*c*) Who is he, and what are his qualifications for making this speech?

Be careful to avoid the two most common mistakes of presiding officers when introducing speakers: (1) Do not make biographical errors. (2) Do not make the introduction too long or overly laudatory. You may be inspired by enthusiasm and admiration, but long tributes are a disservice to a speaker.

Face your audience until you have completed your introduction, so they will hear the speaker's name and subject. Then turn quickly and make a welcoming gesture toward the speaker, at the same time repeating his name. Stay at the lectern until he gets there, greet him, then retire.

When a speaker has finished, always thank him with two or three sentences of appreciative comment.

The program should be a timetable as well as a reminder list of features. No matter how important a speaker may be, there is a courteous way of having an advance understanding about his time allotment. Because the moderator had failed to do this, Vice President Barkley once ran over 15 minutes when he was talking at Town Meeting of the Air over a national radio network, and snarled up the whole program.

A common weakness of program chairmen is to make their schedules too tight. The person who is to preside really should be consulted on this point, since the ultimate responsibility for holding to the timetable will rest upon him.

Dyer, Evans, and Lovell remind us that at least 17 minutes of stretch should be allowed for a session in which four speakers are to participate. Allow 5 minutes to get started, 4 minutes for switching speakers and very briefly introducing them, and 8 minutes for introductory remarks by the speakers, which often cause them to run over their time limits. This is surely a very minimal allowance. It makes two large assumptions: First, that the meeting will start on time; and second, that the introductions can be held to one minute each. And that depends greatly on who's doing the introducing. Give your program enough breathing space.

4. *Adjourning the meeting.* When you adjourn the meeting, be sure that the group is informed of the date, time, and place of the next meeting. If these facts are not available, state that the meeting adjourns subject to the call of the chairman or that the time, place, and date will be announced as the case may be. If there are any acknowledgments and expressions of thanks, make them brief.

Your Conduct as Chairman

These points will help you to acquit yourself favorably and may be considered a statement of etiquette for you as presiding officer.

1. Use your judgment and good taste as to the degree of informality you exercise.

2. If the group is small or the meeting informal, you need not stand up when actively presiding. Otherwise,

stand when you speak, when you are spoken to, when you recognize a speaker, when you state a motion or put it to a vote. Be seated while others are speaking.

To Serve as a Referee

Your important role as referee is summarized by Dr. Smedley in *The Amateur Chairman* thus:

You officiate not as the referee of a prize fight, but as the official of a game in which good judgment and good sportsmanship are the rule. It is your business to see that the meeting is conducted fairly and impartially, and that justice prevails. To do this you must have some knowledge of parliamentary procedure. But be careful to take neither yourself nor your parliamentary law too seriously.

Many chairmen—and members of the meeting—lose sight of the fact that parliamentary procedure is intended to help the business move along in an orderly, fair, and expeditious manner. They wrangle over technicalities and forget the purpose of the meeting. This gives parliamentary procedure a bad name. There is nothing wrong with parliamentary procedure except the shortsightedness of those who abuse it.

The four fundamentals of parliamentary procedure should guide your conduct as presiding officer:
1. Ensure justice and courtesy for all.
2. Do only one thing at a time.
3. The majority rules.
4. The minority has a right to be heard.

Do not burden your memory with too many details of parliamentary practice. There are books on the subject, ranging from *Robert's Rules of Order* to pocket charts for ready reference. (Through the courtesy of Toastmasters International, there is reproduced in these pages a useful pocket-sized chart entitled "Parliamentary Procedure in Action.") In a meeting, if there is no parliamentarian, do not be afraid to delay your ruling while you consult this or a similar chart.

Kinds of Motions and Their Precedence

Motions should be considered in their proper order: (1) privileged motions, (2) subsidiary motions, (3) main motions. (Incidental motions cover a variety of proposals that may be made whenever a situation arises that requires them.)

A privileged motion demands immediate consideration. It is one that does not relate to the pending question but is of such importance that it takes precedence over all other matters. The motion is not debatable. Examples are: motion fixing time at which to adjourn; motion to adjourn; motion to take a recess.

A subsidiary motion modifies or otherwise affects a main motion under consideration.

A main motion brings questions before the meeting for consideration.

What Would You Like to Do?

Introduce business? (A main motion.)

Kill or defer a matter? (Motion to postpone indefinitely: a subsidiary motion.)

Change or modify? (Motion to amend: a subsidiary motion.)

Let a few attend to a matter? (Motion to refer to a committee: a subsidiary motion.)

PARLIAMENTARY PROCEDURE IN ACTION

MOTION	MAY APPLY TO THESE MOTIONS	MAY INTERRUPT A MEMBER ON THE FLOOR	MOVER MUST BE RECOGNIZED	REQUIRES A SECOND	DEBATABLE	VOTE NEEDED
FIX TIME OF NEXT MEETING	NONE	NO	YES	YES	Not when privileged	Majority
TO ADJOURN (Recess)	NONE	NO	YES	YES	Not when privileged	Majority
QUESTION OF PRIVILEGE	NONE	Yes, if necessary	NO	NO	No, but a resulting motion is	Decided by Chair
CALL FOR ORDERS OF THE DAY	Any special or general order	Yes, to call for a special order	NO	NO	NO	None, it takes 2/3 vote to postpone special order
RISE TO POINT OF ORDER	Any motion or act	YES	NO	NO	NO	None, unless appealed, then Majority
APPEAL	Any decision by the Chair	YES	NO	YES	USUALLY NO	Majority
SUSPEND THE RULES	Any motion where needed	NO	YES	YES	NO	Usually 2/3
WITHDRAW (or Renew) A MOTION	Any motion	NO	YES	NO	NO	Majority
OBJECTION TO CONSIDERATION	Main question, and questions of privilege	YES	NO	NO	NO	2/3 in negative

142

LAY ON THE TABLE	Main question, appeals, questions of privilege, reconsideration	NO	YES	YES	NO	Majority
TAKE FROM TABLE	Only to motion that was "tabled"	NO	YES	YES	NO	Majority
CLOSE OR LIMIT DEBATE	Any debatable motion	NO	YES	YES	NO	2/3 Majority
POSTPONE TO CERTAIN DAY	Main motion, questions of privilege, reconsider	NO	YES	YES	YES	Majority
REFER	Main motion, questions of privilege	NO	YES	YES	YES	Majority
AMEND	Main motion, limit debate, refer, postpone definitely, fix time of next meeting	NO	YES	YES	YES	Majority
POSTPONE INDEFINITELY	Main motion, question of privilege	NO	YES	YES	YES	Majority
MAIN QUESTION (or Motion)	No other motion	NO	YES	YES	YES	Majority
RECONSIDER	Any motion except adjourn, suspend rules, lay on table	YES for entry	NO	YES	YES	Majority
RESCIND (or Repeal)	Main motions, appeals, questions of privilege	NO	YES	YES	YES	Majority

Copyright 1961 © Toastmasters International, Inc.

Suspend the rules that interfere with another matter? (Motion to suspend the rules: an incidental motion.)

Things to Remember

1. As chairman, generally you do not enter into discussion. When you must do so, give the chair to another, step down, and ask for recognition. Resume the chair after you have spoken.

2. Always state the exact wording of motions or amendments before a vote.

3. Always indicate clearly how a vote is to be taken. The methods most often used are by voice (call for "aye" or "no"), by show of hands, by rising, and by ballot.

If you are concerned with proxies, mail votes, or other voting questions, consult a good book on parliamentary procedure in advance and take it with you to the meeting.

4. Always call for the negative vote, saying, "Those opposed, say 'No.'"

5. Give each person an opportunity to be heard on a subject before recognizing any speaker for a second time, if possible.

6. Say, "The motion is out of order." Do not say, "You are out of order."

7. When faced with a parliamentary snarl for which you do not know the answer, state the issue simply and fairly and ask the group to tell you what to do by their vote on it.

To Serve as a Toastmaster

As toastmaster, you are the master of ceremonies. Your purpose is pleasure rather than the conduct of a business meeting, and your manner should be suited to the occasion. You are the genial host, introducing your friends on the platform to your friends in the audience and making it easier for them to get acquainted.

You will be a successful toastmaster if you remember to use good manners, good taste, and good humor. When introducing a speaker:

1. Be brief. Bring him on gracefully and let him make the speech.

2. Be courteous. By your words and welcome, put the speaker at his ease. If he gives a poor performance, your program suffers. Help him contribute to the success of the program for which you are responsible. Don't tell a story at his expense.

3. Avoid clichés and repetition. Use variety in presenting each speaker. Don't say, "We have with us . . ." It's pretty obvious that he's there.

After the speaker has finished, allow a moment for audience applause, then express appreciation in a sentence or two. A mere formal "Thank you, Mr. Jones," sounds almost curt. On the other hand, don't comment at length. The audience will do that.

To Serve as a Pinch Hitter

A good program requires careful planning and the efforts of many people. Sooner or later, something is bound to go wrong or something unplanned or unexpected is sure to happen. The audience looks to the toastmaster and usually takes its cue from him before reacting.

Your ability to serve as pinch hitter—to deliver in an emergency—can save the program. Here is where you prove your mettle and impress your audience. The microphone may fail, or the lights may go out. I recall one Toastmasters convention banquet at which the orchestra played "God Save the Queen" before an English speaker was introduced. The audience rose and spontaneously sang "America." (As you know, the tune is the same.) Before the speaker could take affront, the Toastmaster observed that, in singing "America" to the tune of "God Save the Queen," the audience was offering proof that Great Britain and the United States have much in common—even their patriotic songs.

What to Do When the Speaker Fails to Appear

The crisis that probably occurs more often than any other is the failure of a scheduled speaker to appear. Unless you have something to say that is appropriate, timely, and an adequate substitute for the expected presentation, don't attempt to "pinch hit" for the absent speaker. Don't tell stories just to take up the time allotted for his talk. You have no right to shortchange the audience.

The audience is entitled to some comment on the absence of the speaker they were led to believe would address them. If you know the reason for his nonappearance, tell the audience and express regret. The best way to make a pinch hit is to have a good substitute speaker ready. Before every meeting, personally check every speaker or participant: be sure he knows when and where he is to appear; confirm your understanding of the subject or title of his talk; verify the accuracy of your biographical information about him; and make sure he knows the amount of time allotted him.

Have a substitute speaker on hand before every meeting, even though you have been assured all participants expect to appear. Unavoidable, last-minute mishaps occur. It is not difficult to assure your substitute speaker that he is not second choice or playing second fiddle. He should be flattered that you recognize his ability to step into the limelight on short notice and perform well.

If you have no substitute speaker available, you may be able to requisition the audience itself. Select a subject appropriate to the meeting and related to its purpose and call for extemporaneous comments from the floor. As a variant to this procedure, call on two or three members to serve as a panel.

Eight Good Points to Keep in Mind

1. Be prepared. Know what you are to do.
2. Have a definite, detailed plan for the meeting.
3. Know what is to be accomplished.
4. Preside fairly and with good humor.
5. Tactfully keep the meeting on the subject.
6. Remember that your audience can think. Don't try to do all the thinking for them.
7. Focus audience attention on the speaker rather than on yourself.
8. Be prepared for every contingency that can be anticipated.

Summary

In presiding at a meeting you may be asked to fill any one of the following four roles:

1. To serve as pilot. This includes guiding the meeting through all its formal steps in the proper order.

2. To act as referee. In this role your job is to make sure that everyone has a chance to speak in his proper turn while keeping any disagreements that may arise from becoming unpleasant.

3. To serve as toastmaster. As presiding officer it may be your job to introduce any guests and speakers.

4. To pinch hit. Even in the best-run clubs, a program may run into difficulty. Your job is to take care of any emergency ranging from a broken microphone to a delayed or suddenly canceled speaker.

CHAPTER 13

How to Find an Audience

You are one of the most needed people in this country, if you can give a good speech. Because Americans are gregarious, free to express themselves, with the time and means to organize and to congregate, they provide speakers with opportunities to talk on almost any subject, at almost any hour of the day or night, before nearly every kind of audience.

The need is great. Anyone who can satisfy it receives recognition, rewards, and personal satisfaction. In doing your part to meet the demand for good speakers, you will become a better speaker, better qualified to please listeners, with even greater personal compensations for your efforts.

Like athletes, speakers get "rusty" if they do not perform. The best way to become a better speaker is to speak often—and to learn something from each new experience.

You have the know-how and the desire. Where will you find your forum? How should you bring about an invitation?

Who Are Your Potential Listeners?

A recently published directory of national associations in the United States lists more than sixteen thousand agricultural, educational, business, cultural, fraternal, labor, governmental, health, national and ethnic, professional, public affairs, religious, scientific, social welfare, and other organizations. You name it: there's an organization for it. Most of them have local units and hold frequent meetings. Where there are meetings, speakers are needed.

Many years ago, when I was Executive Assistant to the Mayor of Los Angeles, I decided to organize a City Speakers Bureau. I intended to enlist one or two speakers from each of the municipal departments, who would be available to speak to local clubs. Two startling facts compelled me to drop the idea: (1) few city employees were capable of making an effective speech; (2) I learned from the editor of the women's page of one of the local newspapers that she had compiled a list of four thousand women's clubs alone that wanted speakers for their weekly or monthly meetings. In short, the demand far exceeded the supply.

Where to Find an Audience

There are so many clubs, associations, organizations, and special groups that obviously it would be impossible to

list them here, nor is this necessary. All any speaker has to do to find an audience is to ask himself these three questions:
1. Who needs me to speak *for* them?
2. Who needs me to speak *to* them?
3. To whom do I *want* to speak?

1. *Who Needs Me to Speak FOR Them?*

There are many groups with messages of interest and importance that lack skilled speakers to carry their message. Many organizations have available "Speaker's Kits" with useful information and the results of research that no individual speaker has the time or opportunity to develop. Often these organizations receive requests to furnish speakers, and they welcome those who make their abilities known.

One of the best places to begin your inquiry is in the yellow pages of your local telephone directory under "Associations."

The Boy Scouts of America has excellent speaker's kits. Its Civic Relationships division in New Brunswick, New Jersey, is always on the alert for civic leaders and men interested in telling other groups about the Scout movement. Many national organizations in the public health field, such as The National Foundation and the American Cancer Society, have speaker's kits with material ranging from fact sheets to sample speeches. You will probably find that these groups have local chapters or offices.

Join your local Chamber of Commerce. Thousands of local chambers offer three study courses prepared and sponsored by the United States Chamber on "Basic Economics," "Practical Politics," and "Freedom versus Communism." If you enroll in one of these courses, not only will you have something to talk about but many chambers will welcome the opportunity to call on you to fill speaking engagements made available to them.

Identify yourself with the political party of your choice and attend its meetings. You will obtain practice in impromptu speaking; you will be asked to address political meetings; and good speakers are potential candidates for office.

There are reported to be more than 300,000 churches in the United States. Most of them have one or more affiliated groups, such as men's clubs and women's clubs, meeting weekly. Join a church or let your church society officers know of your willingness to participate in a program. You will be welcomed.

If you are a business or professional man, one of your best opportunities rests with the trade or professional organization open to you. If you don't know the organization appropriate for you, drop a note to the American Society of Association Executives, Associations Building, Washington 6, D.C. Every association has a story to tell and needs articulate spokesmen to communicate with the public. Every association member is a public relations representative of his industry or profession. Association executives are eager to find speakers as well as speaking opportunities for them.

I strongly recommend that you join a Toastmasters or Toastmistress club and qualify for its Speakers Bureau. More and more Toastmasters clubs now provide speakers for other groups, after their own members qualify for the assignments offered them. Toastmasters clubs do not tell you what to say; they do give you advice and the privilege of practicing and then provide opportunities to "speak your own mind" before others.

2. Who Needs Me to Speak TO Them?

Audiences in search of speakers exceed the supply of those capable of appearing on programs. Find a club, and you've found a forum. Although some large organizations compensate program speakers, most clubs have no funds for the purpose. They are grateful to speakers who are willing to appear without cost to the group. Under the circumstances, club program chairmen are not too exacting as to speech topics. They require only that the speaker be able to speak well; and that, of course, includes the ability to interest an audience. As I pointed out in an earlier chapter, you should select a subject of probable interest to your audience, but most service clubs and women's clubs do not ask that you speak in a special area or on a topic of their selection.

Your local newspaper is the most fruitful source of information. All papers report meetings of clubs and organizations. Note the organization, the subject of the talks reported, and especially the name of any club officer listed. Give careful attention to the women's page, where you will find accounts of a variety of women's club meetings. Other helpful sources of audience information are the office of your mayor and your congressman. They will usually be glad to suggest groups for you to get in touch with.

3. To Whom Do I WANT to Speak?

The speaker in search of an audience must use a slightly different approach from that of the speaker whose own organization constitutes his audience. The requirements are usually simple, however.

You must let representatives of the audience you have selected know that you want to talk to them. Don't be shy or falsely modest about your availability. You have something they want. On the other hand, don't puff your wares or be boastful. An informal, direct phone call or letter of inquiry to a club officer or program chairman will nearly always establish the necessary contact. State your understanding that the group sometimes has a speaker on its program from outside the membership, and indicate that you would consider it a privilege if they would care to have you appear. State the subjects on which you are competent to speak and ask what subject the club would prefer.

To accredit yourself, mention some of the groups you have addressed and the subjects you presented and invite your contact to get in touch with named representatives of these groups to learn how they received your talk. If you have some special qualifications, state these. Perhaps you have just returned from a trip to Honduras, and you believe the club might be interested in hearing about women's fashions or the status of women there. If you haven't traveled recently and you operate a filling station or a dress shop in addition to your avocation as a speaker, you may be brave enough to talk on "How My Women Customers Look to Me." And be sure to mention that since public speaking is your avocation, or since you appreciate the opportunity to present your particular message, you are glad to appear without any fee.

If you speak well before several groups, you will find that they will speak well of you to others and that unsolicited opportunities will come your way.

After you have made enough appearances to gain at least a small local reputation and have developed several talks of proved interest, you may wish to compose a small folder announcing your availability. This should be brief and businesslike. Show your picture. This will identify you when you go to the meeting. If you limit yourself on subject matter, state the titles of your talks, with a sentence or two describing your presentation. With their permission, list some of the groups to whom you have spoken. And don't forget to give your address or phone number. Your folder ought to be of such dimensions that it will fit easily into a No. 10 correspondence envelope, for convenience in mailing. Any neighborhood printer can meet your needs, and the cost is very modest.

Special Opportunities for Women Speakers

You may be surprised to learn that women probably have more opportunities to speak in public than men have. There are not so many women who are good speakers and have something to say. There are many organizations that seek women as speakers just because they *are* women. There are still more groups that want speakers regardless of sex. Because many men are not available, especially during business hours, women speakers obtain opportunities by default, and win additional opportunities because they have demonstrated their abilities.

Opportunities for women speakers are so numerous, and requirements so varied and diverse at the local level, that only general leads can be suggested here. However, a half hour of effort should lead any woman to so many prospective audiences that an attractive list of choices will confront her.

Generally speaking, opportunities for women fall into three broad categories:

a) Organizations a woman can join that provide opportunities to speak within the group.

b) Organizations that seek recruits for their Speakers Bureaus, or that provide materials, instruction, and speaking engagements on their behalf, before other groups.

c) Groups that seek outside speakers.

The National Women Accountants' Association is one of hundreds of organizations interested in obtaining women speakers just because they *are* women, or because they are active in special fields of interest to the audience. Mrs. Kay Fields, executive of a large real estate holding corporation and Vice-President of the Orange County, California, chapter of NWAA, says: "As Chairman of our Program Committee, I am always on the lookout for women to speak to our chapter. Our members are particularly interested in what women speakers have to say, especially if they are accountants or in related activities. However, we have had several women outside these fields speak to us about equal pay for women and special problems of women in business and professional work."

The General Federation of Women's Clubs, 1734 N Street, N.W., Washington, D.C., is one of the largest organizations of women. It has a membership of 11,000,000 women in 53 countries. In the United States there are 800,000 members in 15,600 clubs affiliated with the parent organization. In each club, members have opportunities to speak, and many of the clubs provide opportunities for their members to speak before outside groups.

The National Federation of Business and Professional Women's Clubs, 2012 Massachusetts Ave., N.W., Washington 6, D.C., has a total membership of 175,000 women in 53 state groups and 3,560 local units. Organized to promote the interests and elevate the standards of business and professional women, it extends their opportunities through education in industrial, scientific, and vocational activities. In fact, many chapters not only provide program opportunities at their own meetings, but also refer outside speaking opportunities to their members.

Zonta International, 59 East Van Buren St., Chicago 5, Illinois, is a service club of women executives in business and the professions. Zonta has nearly 500 local clubs scattered throughout the United States alone. These clubs provide speaking opportunities for their members on their own programs and many of the clubs encourage their members to speak before other groups that call on Zonta for speakers.

Women United for United Nations, 345 East 46th Street, New York 17, New York, represents 52 national, nongovernmental organizations of women. It disseminates information to familiarize the public with United Nations' activities and provides program ideas for use in local chapters of various organizations. It is a splendid source of information on speech materials and organizations with Speakers Bureaus, for women interested in the varied and extensive activities of the United Nations and its affiliated agencies.

Local chapters of national organizations in the health and medical fields are constantly seeking speakers for their year-'round public information programs and for their fund-raising activities.

The American Cancer Society, 219 East 42nd Street, New York City, has 3,100 local units and will refer you to the chapter nearest you. The National Association for Mental Health, 10 Columbus Circle, New York 19, New York, has nearly 1,000 local units. The National Foundation, 800 2nd Avenue, New York 17, New York, works largely through other organizations, but an inquiry to its staff headquarters will bring you much helpful information.

Don't overlook the trade associations and commercial organizations. Members of these groups want practical points directly related to their business activity, and they don't care about the sex of the speaker. Recently I called the office of the National Restaurant Association, 1530 North Lake Shore Drive, Chicago 10, Illinois. I said I represented an experienced woman speaker who wanted to talk on "What Women Look for in Restaurants" or "Why Women Like to Eat Out." I was referred to several local restaurant associations within driving distance of my home, and received some very helpful educational material a few days later by mail.

"What Women Dislike about Car Salesmen" was offered as a speech topic to a regional motor-car dealers association. The owner of the auto agency, to whom the topic was suggested, called one of the association officers immediately, and was assured that the prospective speaker would be invited to talk at the next association meeting.

Membership—The Best Opportunity

The greatest opportunities for a woman to speak in public and, more important, to satisfy her need to feel needed by others, rests in participating membership in one of the many organizations for women.

Many women overlook the opportunity because they still hold the old-fashioned notion that a "clubwoman" is an ineffective, middle-aged woman who attends teas, fashion shows, or lecture groups in a desperate effort to escape boredom.

This is no longer true. Ellen Shulte, writing in the *Los Angeles Times* for Sunday, October 4, 1964, says, " 'Clubwoman' is an image that needs updating." In her article, Miss Shulte quotes Mrs. Robert Newman, Vice-President of the California League of Women Voters as saying: "It's time to put a serious, meaningful interpretation to the term 'clubwoman.' The term now has a frivolous connotation and it's out of step with modern women's group activities."

This view is endorsed by Mrs. David Menkin, U.C.L.A. instructor of community workshops for club and organization members, who is quoted as saying: "I find that even groups which started out strictly as social groups have turned their attention toward philanthropic or civic work. And these women don't want to be considered as frivolous."

Mrs. Laura F. Curry, President of the Los Angeles Metropolitan District of the California Federation of Women's Clubs, says that the district theme for the year, "New Horizons in the Field of Service," indicates the trend. The California Federation of Women's Clubs was comprised only of reading and entertainment groups when it was founded in 1900. Today it has 67,000 members in 828 clubs throughout the state, working on a variety of educational and service projects, with cultural and community improvement as a goal.

The California League of Women Voters has 12,000 members and wants more. This nonpartisan organization, like other state-affiliated units of the National League of Women Voters, is dedicated to informing the public about government and current political issues. It prints and distributes literature and holds study groups for members and nonmembers, and its Los Angeles League participates in television programs to present pros and cons in election periods.

Mrs. Sidney Melford, active in the organization, reports that women who are effective public speakers can find plenty of opportunities in LWV.

Where to Look for Other Opportunities

For the woman who doesn't want to confine her speaking to one group through membership participation in its program, there are several fruitful starting points in looking for audiences.

1. Public library—Go to your public library and look for a compilation of organizations. Your librarian will help you. Perhaps the most complete reference source is *Encyclopedia of Associations* (4th Edition), a two-volume directory of more than 12,500 organizations. Published by the Gale Research Company, Book Tower, Detroit, Michigan, these volumes carry detailed listings and indexes according to the nature of the organization, as well as by location and by identification of organization executives.

2. Women's editor, your local paper—In most instances you will find that the women's editor of your newspaper has a fund of information on women's clubs, and she prob-

ably knows which groups seek outside speakers and which clubs have speakers bureaus. If you prefer not to call her, become a daily reader of the women's page of the paper. You will soon be able to compile a list of clubs, names of program chairmen, and you will acquire information as to the subjects and types of speakers in which local groups are interested.

3. Mayor's office—Every Mayor receives more invitations to speak than he can satisfy. In many cities, someone in the Mayor's office keeps a list of organizations that have asked the Mayor or other city officials to address their membership. Most of the larger cities have a city information officer, who usually has this material. Your city officials are usually very helpful in making suggestions if you visit their office, state the nature of your inquiry, and satisfy them as to your qualifications.

A Word of Caution

Your stated interest in finding an audience will rarely be sufficient to bring you an invitation. You must learn all you can about an organization, its purposes, the interests of its membership, and the kinds of subjects it wants to hear about. You must also satisfy the program chairman that you are an experienced speaker, by referring to other groups you have addressed, and by stating your qualifications for consideration.

Good luck!

Summary

Once you have developed your potential as a speaker, there are several ways in which you can find audiences.

To start with, you should decide which groups need you to speak *for* them, which need you to speak *to* them, and which you *want* to address.

Among groups who can either invite you to speak or direct you to an audience are national philanthropic associations, local Chambers of Commerce, service clubs, political organizations, churches, and Toastmasters.

To gain invitations, you may get in touch with specific prospects, listing your qualifications. Eventually you may even wish to assemble a folder discussing your previous engagements and indicating your fields of interest.

If you are a woman, be sure to take advantage of the many organizations interested in finding competent women speakers.

CHAPTER 14

How to Talk to a Service Club

MEN's service clubs provide the best audiences and offer the most rewarding opportunities for good speakers.

As America's unique contribution to good fellowship and the welfare of mankind, our service clubs have spread to all the free countries in the world. These organizations have earned universal acceptance because they provide men with enjoyable companionship and the opportunity for voluntary cooperation in rendering personal service to their community and their neighbors in need. Men's service clubs are growing in membership, in local, national, and international influence, in the value of their contributions to their fellow men, and in the recognition they give to those who qualify for leadership in their affairs.

What do they offer to public speakers? Lions, Rotary,

Kiwanis, Optimist, and Sertoma are five of the leaders among dozens of national and international service groups. The total membership of these five is more than a million and a half; they represent nearly forty thousand local clubs, which meet from two to four times a month. Most of these meetings have outside speakers, and every meeting of every club provides opportunities for the member who wants to speak up. Each of these clubs also sponsors one or more projects of benefit to the community and to those in need of help. There is always an urgent need for those who can explain or inform or stir public interest and support for these activities.

Toastmasters International, like its sister organization, Toastmistresses, is more than a service club in that its units also provide training in public speaking and group leadership. So many Toastmasters have applied their skills in becoming more effective leaders in other organizations that one association executive recently told me, "Toastmasters may not be primarily a service club, but it certainly provides a service to service clubs."

To meet the need for public speaking ability on the part of their officers, many service clubs encourage their rising leaders to become Toastmasters.

Effective public speakers are needed (1) for club program talks, (2) to speak on behalf of club service projects, and (3) to become leaders within the service club.

John H. Vogt, Executive Administrator of Lions International, and himself a one-time Toastmasters club president, says:

Obtaining a continuing supply of challenging, interesting speakers is a problem for all but the largest metropolitan clubs, and the Program Committee—whose task it is to maintain membership interest through good speakers and programs—is usually the hardest working committee in the club's organization.

Mr. Vogt speaks with authority. His association is the largest and one of the most highly regarded of all men's service club organizations. There are 700,000 Lions in more than 17,500 clubs in 122 countries. All follow the established pattern of service club meetings: the preliminaries of song, pledge of allegiance, and invocation, a luncheon or dinner, club announcements and discussion, and then the meeting program. This usually consists of a talk by an outside speaker.

The Lions Club audience is similar to that of the other service clubs. Mr. Vogt says:

Members of Lions Clubs are business and professional men in the community. Most of them are civic leaders, active in the governmental, school, church, and business life of their towns. They are banded together in the Lions Club because they know that forty or fifty men, working together, can produce more ideas and action than a thousand men working as individuals. Lions International, as a unifying organization of their clubs, supplies information, direction and ideas to help them do a better job. But to a great extent these men depend upon informed, interesting speakers to keep them alert to the problems, developments and needs of their communities, their nations and their world.

To give readers of this book authoritative advice on how to talk to service clubs, I solicited the counsel of three of the ablest service club executives in this country: John H. Vogt, from whose specially prepared statement I have already quoted; Bernard B. Burford, Secretary-Treasurer, Optimist International; and Richard C. Murray, Managing Director, Sertoma International.

What type of speaker does a service club seek? According to Mr. Vogt:

Not the flamboyant, flag-waving, canned speech orator. Most Lions are grass-roots people who can spot sham and hypocrisy in a speech a mile off. Neither do they want the soporific mumbler—the man who is up to his ears in his subject, but hems and haws through a cliché-ridden sermon that makes the members wish they had stayed home!

Mr. Vogt expresses the listener attitude of all service club members when he observes:

We don't expect a Billy Graham at every meeting, but neither do we stand for speakers who pay no dividends for the investment of our time. A poor speaker hurts our intelligence; too many of them can hurt attendance. We look for speakers who have something worthwhile to tell us, who leave us with something to think about, and who have at least enough platform presence to keep the fellows in the back rows from walking out.

Richard C. Murray offers some detailed tips to help speakers establish rapport with their service club audience and observes that this is an area in which many speakers fail.

"Inquire ahead of time as to the club's achievements and any projects with which it is identified in the community," says Mr. Murray, adding, "This can be done during the meal preceding your speech if you are good with the ad lib."

There is danger to the speaker who fails to inform himself, Mr. Murray points out.

A speaker who fails to do this misses the boat for a natural bridge to his audience. I have seen speakers talk on a theme which was almost identical to one of the club's own activities or projects, and fail to mention them. When the club's activity can be linked with the point the speaker is making, the point itself is driven home with great emphasis to the listeners.

Mr. Murray emphasizes that usually more than half of any service club audience is made up of habitual attendants, most of whom listen to fifty-two luncheon speakers a year. The personal touch, referring to distinguished members of the club, mentioning its achievements, and a concluding expression of good wishes or statement of your hopes for the club's success in its particular endeavor make the members appreciate your interest in them and remember you happily.

Best Subjects for Service Clubs

Speaking for his membership, Mr. Vogt says:

Basically our Lions Clubs want speakers who will talk *with* them—not *at* them—about their favorite cooperative subject— service to their community and its people. Lions will listen intently to a speaker on any phase of community improvement, better municipal government, better civic spirit, industrial or rural development, improved health or social service. They will listen with interest to any talk on better schools. They will pay strict attention to arresting messages on safety, taxation, better police service, improved facilities for the young people of their towns. A favorite topic is travel. I have attended Lions meetings at which the speaker discussed the dope evil, better television programs, brighter street lighting, the operation of the stock market, and the establishment of a community hospital. While Lions enjoy an occasional "happy talk," they hew pretty close to the line of service and prefer a speaker with a message rather than a lot of belly laughs.

Each year Bernard B. Burford, Secretary-Treasurer of Optimist International, emphasizes the importance of public speaking as an aid to new club officers and district governors of his organization. Mr. Burford offers a suggestion that will serve well any speaker who seeks advancement within any service club organization.

At our Annual Governor's Conference I tell our officers that during the coming year they will need three types of talks. One would be a *prepared* extemporaneous one to fit all occasions. The second would deal with the philosophy of our organization, and the third would be strictly shop talk based on "How To" accomplish our objectives and programs.

Mr. Burford has given me permission to quote the following guides that he offers to Optimist officers seeking his advice on how to talk to Optimist Clubs. The suggestions should be taken to heart by all speakers.

1. Never start your speech with an apology. You need not warn your listeners they are going to be bored. They'll find out soon enough.
2. Don't exaggerate—you gain nothing.
3. Avoid sarcasm to anyone and anything. Avoid the joke with a sting or a double meaning.
4. Don't murder the English language.
5. Avoid shady material.
6. Avoid being too sentimental—pathos isn't appreciated.

7. Try not to be dull—it shows a lack of preparation.
8. Don't wander from your subject—you weaken your speech.
9. Express yourself concisely, clearly, and completely.
10. Keep statistics at a minimum. They are dull and your listeners will not remember most of them.
11. Have mercy on your audience; don't be long-winded.

The adjuration to speak briefly is echoed by Mr. Vogt, who offers this advice on how long to talk to any service club.

Twenty minutes should be the limit for noon meetings, which are taken out of a busy day and are usually compact and fast moving. At evening meetings, thirty minutes is the maximum. Usually the speaker is told in advance, but if he isn't, there is one reliable rule: when more than one listener pulls out his watch, sit down.

George Means, General Secretary of Rotary International, shares the view emphasized by Messrs. Vogt, Burford, and Murray that successful service club speakers should cooperate with the club's program chairman. He will probably introduce you, so give him some material to work with. And by all means be on time—which means that you should arrive at least fifteen minutes before the meeting opens.

Lions, Rotary, Kiwanis, Optimist, Sertoma—and dozens of organizations I cannot cite because of space limitations—all are eager for interesting, competent speakers. As John Vogt says, "They provide a ready-made intelligent, challenging audience for anyone who has a worthwhile message. Don't wait for an invitation. Offer your services as a speaker, providing you have something to say."

You should have little trouble establishing contact with your local service clubs. You may not find them in the telephone directory, but your Chamber of Commerce or your local newspaper can usually give you the necessary information. From time to time reports of speeches at club meetings appear in your paper, and the name of a club officer is usually in the story. Make yourself known to him; state your qualifications and what you would like to talk about, and you will receive serious consideration in almost every instance. If you make it clear that you expect no fee, this will be of added interest.

You will get at least as much out of your talk to the club as your listeners will get from you. Service clubs are among your best audiences.

Index

Accent, 96, 102, 103
Active vs. passive voice, 68
Adams, John Chester, 14
Addressing, forms of, 54
Adjectives and adverbs, 73
American Cancer Society, 151, 158
American Society of Assn. Executives, 152
Amiel, Henri Frédéric, 18
Apologies, to be avoided, 56
Arrangements for speech, 11
Attention-arresting, 55
Audience, appraisal, 7
   basic wants, 119
   culture patterns, 118
   church, 152
   eye support, 41
   effect desired, 112
   information on, 11
   how to find one, 149–150
   lack of response, 126
   make appeals specific, 123
   service clubs, 163–170
   underdog questioners, 131
   viewpoint, 20, 23

Barkley, Alben, 138
Barton, Clara, 51
Beginners, advice to, 3
Beliefs carelessly formed, 120
Bender, James H., on voice, 102
Bevan, Aneurin, 73
Bismarck, Otto, 112
Books, reference, 75–76
   for source material, 30–31
Boy Scouts of America, 151
Bryan, William Jennings, 19
Bryant, Muriel, on dress, 85
Buford, Bernard B., 166, 168
Butterflies in stomach, 3

Calif. Fed. Women's Clubs, 159
   League Women voters, 159
   State College, Fullerton, California, 71
Chalk talk, 89

Chamber of Commerce, 151
  St. Louis, 80
Chamber of Commerce, U.S., 151
Chronological sequence, 51
Churchill, Winston, preparation, 36
Civil Liberties Union, 117
Clarity, first objective, 71
Clergymen, mannerisms, 99
Clichés, 77
Color in a speech, 74
Curry, Mrs. Laura F., 159

DeArmond, Fred, on speech topics, 24
Demonstrations, 91
Dental Hygienists Society, 13
Dewey, Thos. E., 102
Dignity, when to forget, 79
Dress for a speaker, 85
Dyer, Evans, and Lovell, 139

Einstein, Albert, 19
Eloquence, its prerequisites, 19
Encyclopedia of Associations, 160
English usage references, 76

Fear, how to minimize, 3
Feelings, conceal the negative, 6
Ferguson, Chas. W., on clarity, 77
Fessenden, Seth A., vii
Fields, Kay, 156
Figurative speech, 77
Flash cards, 88
Flesch, Rudolph, readability, 73
Flip charts, 88
Funk, Wilfred, 106
Funston, Keith, 80

Gen. Fed. of Women's Clubs, 156
Geneva convention, 51

Ghost-writing, 78
Gibbons, Floyd, 96
Guide to Personal Successs in Management, 24

Hamlet, 107, 117
Hamilton, Alex., transition, 67
Hayden, Sheldon, on subject matter, 13
Harte, Bret, spoke out of character, 19
Hegarty, Edward, on ghosting, 79
Hemingway, Ernest, 107
Hiroshima, 51
Hobbies, as speech topic, 20
Hoover, Herbert, 19
Hope, Bob, 19
Housewife, topics for, 31
Hubbard, Elbert, no apology, 56
Hull, John E., 80
Humor, misplaced, 12

Impromptu speaking, 34
Indirect approach, 120
Inflection of voice, 102
International Red Cross, 51
Introduction, acknowledgment, 11, 54
Introduction of speaker, 138
Inventory of information, 28

Johnson, Hugh, 130
Johnson, Lyndon B., 112
  style, 68
Jones, Paul, on statistics, 70

Kaltenborn, H. V., radio talks, 36
Kiwanis International, 164

Lapp, Chas. L., showmanship, 91
Leosthenes, 112

Lecterns, 83
Letter confirming speech date, 15
Lewis, Hazel Leona, xiv
Library of Congress, 51–52
Libraries, tips on using, 31
Lighting for projectors, 91
Lincoln, Abraham, 103
Listener viewpoint, 23
Listener's interest first, 46
Lions' International, 164, 168
Los Angeles Speakers Bureau, 150
Los Angeles Times, 159

Makeup for a speaker, 86–87
Mann, Evelyn, on dress, 85
Manuscripts to be read, 40, 41, 66
Martin, Joe, down East accent, 96
   manuscript, 40
Massoth, Clifford G., 78
Means, George, 169
Memorize your speech? 39
Memory aids, 42
   blocks to remembrance, 43
   conscious effort, 46
   devices for prompting, 44
   frequency, intensity, recency, 42, 43
Menkin, Mrs. David, 159
Merman, Ethel, on fear, 6
Michaels, Chas. Jr., use of notes, 38
Microphone use, 84
Milford, Mrs. Sidney, 160
Miller, Helen, use of notes, 43
Misquotations, danger of, 33
Morrow, Dwight, on clarity, 72
Morton, Thruston, parenthetical expressions, 69
Movies, 89
Murray, Richard C., 166

Musey, George J., xiv
Myers, Geo. I., pulpit gymnastics, 98

NAACP, 117
National Assn. of Mfrs., 114
Nat'l Assn. for Mental Health, 158
Nat'l Fed. Business and Prof. Women's Clubs, 157
National Foundation, 151, 158
National Restaurant Assn., 158
National Safety Council, 70
National Women Accountants' Assn., 156
Nervousness is normal, 3
Newman, Mrs. Robt., 159
Newspapers as sources, 153
New York Stock Exchange, 80
Nightingale, Florence, 51
Northwestern University, 72
Note-taking procedure, 32
Notes, ways of using, 42

Occasions for speeches, 11
Oliver, Robert T., 7
Opdycke, John B., 77
Opinion molding, 110
Optimist International, 166
Order of business, 135–137
Organizations that need speakers, 150
Order of arranging material, 51–52
   of importance in outline, 52
Osler, William, 102
Outline in organizing a talk, 49
Outline sequence, 48, 49

PAIL opening formula, 54
Parenthetical expressions, 69
Parent Teachers Assn., 69
Parliamentary procedure, 140, 141
   in action, 142–143

173

Persuasion principles, 114
Plutarch on Leosthenes, 112
Posture for a speaker, 86
Presiding at a meeting, 134
  role of presiding officer, 135; when speaker fails to appear, 146
Program schedule, 137–138
Problem-solution formula, 113; sequence, 53
Properties for demonstrations, 91
  stage, 91
Public library use, 160
Publicity releases, 80

Q.E.D. in outline, 59
Questions asked speakers, 125
  brevity in answers, 127
  courtesy to questioners, 129
  how to end, 132
  how to stimulate, 126
  loaded against speaker, 130
  recognizing questioners, 128
  to be repeated, 128
Quotations, use of, 57

Reading aloud, 40
Recorded sound, 89
Reference sources, 31–32
Rehearsals, 44–45
  for timing, 60
Rhetorical questions, 58
Robert's Rules of Order, 140
Robinson, Jas. Harvey, 120
Roethlisberger, F. J., 72
Rogers, Will, 19
Roosevelt, Franklin, 4
Rotary International, 169
Royal Bank of Canada, 41

Sanitary Commission, 51
Santa Monica Junior College, 13
Senior Citizens Club, 13
Sentences, short, 68
Sertoma International, 166

Service Clubs, how to talk to, 163
  interests, 116
  their contribution, 163
Showmanship, 91
Shulte, Ellen, 159
Simplicity, 72
  vs. simplification, 77
Slang expressions, 75
Slide presentation, 87
Smedley, Ralph C.
  advice to beginners, 1
  The Amateur Chairman, 135, 140
  antidote to fear, 8
  deplores shouting, 98
Smetka, Alex, xiv
  travel talks, 21
Smith, Al, 96
Social Security, 121
Sources of information, 160–161
Spatial order of material, 51
Speaker, his ego, 4
Speaker, assets, 1; born or made, 1; identification with audience, 115–116; make yourself available, 154; pinch hitter, 145; women, 85–86, 99–100, 108, 155–160
Speech essentials, 18
  3 classifications, 34
Speech, and conversation, 69
  blueprint for, 48
  collaboration, 45
  conclusion, six types, 57
  examples of accent, 103
  extempore, 34–37
  formal, 38–44
  impromptu, 34–35
  notes and reminders, 37
  openings, 54–56
  organizing, 49, 113
  practice, 41
  rehearsals, 44–55
  releases, 79

speed of speaking, 106
versus essay, 66
Spurgeon, Chas. H., 97
Stage-setting, 83
Statistics, their use, 70, 87
Stevenson, R. L., 106–107
Style, the conversational, 68
Subject of speech, 16
    to auto salesmen, 158
    too broad, 27
    cooking and foods, 30
    experiences from daily life, 30
    file, diary, etc., 18
    research, 27
    travel, 167
Summary close, 57
Surprise Symphony, 97

Thesaurus, how to use, 76
Thoreau, Henry, on fear, 4
    travel in Concord, 21
Time allotment, 14
Times, New York, Index, 32
Timing a speech, 59, 60
    avoid speed-up, 62
    time curtailment, 61
    length flexibility, 60–61
    in rehearsal, 60
Toastmasters clubs, 152
Toastmasters International, 1, 164
Toastmaster magazine, 7, 38
Toastmaster function, 143, 144
Toastmistress clubs, 30, 152
Toastmistress magazine, 85
Topic selections, 19
Transitions, between topics, 67
Travel as speech topics, 20, 167
    what to look for, 21
Twain, Mark, 19
    impromptu speaking, 35

United Nations, 157
University of Calif., L.A., 159

Visual aids, 87–90
    7 rules, 90–91
Vocabulary value, 74
Vogt, John H., 164, 169
Voice, and accent, 102
    check list, 109
    change of pace, 9
    to be cultivated, 104
    and diaphragm, 108
    distinctions, 95–96
    and emotions, 97
    evaluation questionnaire, 105
    modulation, 102
    pitch, 99
    time, 100–101
    volume, 98
    weaknesses, 105
    women's, 96

Webster, Daniel, 56
Who, what, where, how, why? 17
Winchell, Walter, 96
Women, audiences, 154
    clubs, 156–160
    cooking and foods, 30
    as speakers, 85–86, 99–100, 108, 155–160
    tips on topics, 22
    United for U.N., 157
Word finders, 32, 76
Words, choice, 74
    facility, 75
    mispronounced, 104
    10 most beautiful, 106
Wren, Christopher, audibility, 40
Writing makes a better speech, 66

Yale University Debate Team, 14

Zonta International, 157

MELVIN POWERS SELF-IMPROVEMENT LIBRARY

ASTROLOGY
____ ASTROLOGY: HOW TO CHART YOUR HOROSCOPE *Max Heindel*	3.00
____ ASTROLOGY: YOUR PERSONAL SUN-SIGN GUIDE *Beatrice Ryder*	3.00
____ ASTROLOGY FOR EVERYDAY LIVING *Janet Harris*	2.00
____ ASTROLOGY MADE EASY *Astarte*	3.00
____ ASTROLOGY MADE PRACTICAL *Alexandra Kayhle*	3.00
____ ASTROLOGY, ROMANCE, YOU AND THE STARS *Anthony Norvell*	4.00
____ MY WORLD OF ASTROLOGY *Sydney Omarr*	5.00
____ THOUGHT DIAL *Sidney Omarr*	4.00
____ WHAT THE STARS REVEAL ABOUT THE MEN IN YOUR LIFE *Thelma White*	3.00

BRIDGE
____ BRIDGE BIDDING MADE EASY *Edwin B. Kantar*	7.00
____ BRIDGE CONVENTIONS *Edwin B. Kantar*	7.00
____ BRIDGE HUMOR *Edwin B. Kantar*	5.00
____ COMPETITIVE BIDDING IN MODERN BRIDGE *Edgar Kaplan*	4.00
____ DEFENSIVE BRIDGE PLAY COMPLETE *Edwin B. Kantar*	10.00
____ GAMESMAN BRIDGE—Play Better with Kantar *Edwin B. Kantar*	5.00
____ HOW TO IMPROVE YOUR BRIDGE *Alfred Sheinwold*	5.00
____ IMPROVING YOUR BIDDING SKILLS *Edwin B. Kantar*	4.00
____ INTRODUCTION TO DECLARER'S PLAY *Edwin B. Kantar*	5.00
____ INTRODUCTION TO DEFENDER'S PLAY *Edwin B. Kantar*	3.00
____ KANTAR FOR THE DEFENSE *Edwin B. Kantar*	5.00
____ SHORT CUT TO WINNING BRIDGE *Alfred Sheinwold*	3.00
____ TEST YOUR BRIDGE PLAY *Edwin B. Kantar*	5.00
____ VOLUME 2—TEST YOUR BRIDGE PLAY *Edwin B. Kantar*	5.00
____ WINNING DECLARER PLAY *Dorothy Hayden Truscott*	4.00

BUSINESS, STUDY & REFERENCE
____ CONVERSATION MADE EASY *Elliot Russell*	3.00
____ EXAM SECRET *Dennis B. Jackson*	3.00
____ FIX-IT BOOK *Arthur Symons*	2.00
____ HOW TO DEVELOP A BETTER SPEAKING VOICE *M. Hellier*	3.00
____ HOW TO MAKE A FORTUNE IN REAL ESTATE *Albert Winnikoff*	4.00
____ INCREASE YOUR LEARNING POWER *Geoffrey A. Dudley*	3.00
____ MAGIC OF NUMBERS *Robert Tocquet*	2.00
____ PRACTICAL GUIDE TO BETTER CONCENTRATION *Melvin Powers*	3.00
____ PRACTICAL GUIDE TO PUBLIC SPEAKING *Maurice Forley*	5.00
____ 7 DAYS TO FASTER READING *William S. Schaill*	3.00
____ SONGWRITERS' RHYMING DICTIONARY *Jane Shaw Whitfield*	5.00
____ SPELLING MADE EASY *Lester D. Basch & Dr. Milton Finkelstein*	3.00
____ STUDENT'S GUIDE TO BETTER GRADES *J. A. Rickard*	3.00
____ TEST YOURSELF—Find Your Hidden Talent *Jack Shafer*	3.00
____ YOUR WILL & WHAT TO DO ABOUT IT *Attorney Samuel G. Kling*	4.00

CALLIGRAPHY
____ ADVANCED CALLIGRAPHY *Katherine Jeffares*	7.00
____ CALLIGRAPHER'S REFERENCE BOOK *Anne Leptich & Jacque Evans*	7.00
____ CALLIGRAPHY—The Art of Beautiful Writing *Katherine Jeffares*	7.00
____ CALLIGRAPHY FOR FUN & PROFIT *Anne Leptich & Jacque Evans*	7.00
____ CALLIGRAPHY MADE EASY *Tina Serafini*	7.00

CHESS & CHECKERS
____ BEGINNER'S GUIDE TO WINNING CHESS *Fred Reinfeld*	4.00
____ CHECKERS MADE EASY *Tom Wiswell*	2.00
____ CHESS IN TEN EASY LESSONS *Larry Evans*	3.00
____ CHESS MADE EASY *Milton L. Hanauer*	3.00
____ CHESS PROBLEMS FOR BEGINNERS *edited by Fred Reinfeld*	2.00
____ CHESS SECRETS REVEALED *Fred Reinfeld*	2.00
____ CHESS STRATEGY—An Expert's Guide *Fred Reinfeld*	2.00
____ CHESS TACTICS FOR BEGINNERS *edited by Fred Reinfeld*	3.00
____ CHESS THEORY & PRACTICE *Morry & Mitchell*	2.00
____ HOW TO WIN AT CHECKERS *Fred Reinfeld*	3.00
____ 1001 BRILLIANT WAYS TO CHECKMATE *Fred Reinfeld*	4.00

___ 1001 WINNING CHESS SACRIFICES & COMBINATIONS *Fred Reinfeld*	4.00
___ SOVIET CHESS *Edited by R. G. Wade*	3.00

COOKERY & HERBS

___ CULPEPER'S HERBAL REMEDIES *Dr. Nicholas Culpeper*	3.00
___ FAST GOURMET COOKBOOK *Poppy Cannon*	2.50
___ GINSENG The Myth & The Truth *Joseph P. Hou*	3.00
___ HEALING POWER OF HERBS *May Bethel*	4.00
___ HEALING POWER OF NATURAL FOODS *May Bethel*	4.00
___ HERB HANDBOOK *Dawn MacLeod*	3.00
___ HERBS FOR COOKING AND HEALING *Dr. Donald Law*	2.00
___ HERBS FOR HEALTH—How to Grow & Use Them *Louise Evans Doole*	3.00
___ HOME GARDEN COOKBOOK—Delicious Natural Food Recipes *Ken Kraft*	3.00
___ MEDICAL HERBALIST *edited by Dr. J. R. Yemm*	3.00
___ NATURAL FOOD COOKBOOK *Dr. Harry C. Bond*	3.00
___ NATURE'S MEDICINES *Richard Lucas*	3.00
___ VEGETABLE GARDENING FOR BEGINNERS *Hugh Wiberg*	2.00
___ VEGETABLES FOR TODAY'S GARDENS *R. Milton Carleton*	2.00
___ VEGETARIAN COOKERY *Janet Walker*	4.00
___ VEGETARIAN COOKING MADE EASY & DELECTABLE *Veronica Vezza*	3.00
___ VEGETARIAN DELIGHTS—A Happy Cookbook for Health *K. R. Mehta*	2.00
___ VEGETARIAN GOURMET COOKBOOK *Joyce McKinnel*	3.00

GAMBLING & POKER

___ ADVANCED POKER STRATEGY & WINNING PLAY *A. D. Livingston*	5.00
___ HOW NOT TO LOSE AT POKER *Jeffrey Lloyd Castle*	3.00
___ HOW TO WIN AT DICE GAMES *Skip Frey*	3.00
___ HOW TO WIN AT POKER *Terence Reese & Anthony T. Watkins*	3.00
___ SECRETS OF WINNING POKER *George S. Coffin*	3.00
___ WINNING AT CRAPS *Dr. Lloyd T. Commins*	3.00
___ WINNING AT GIN *Chester Wander & Cy Rice*	3.00
___ WINNING AT POKER—An Expert's Guide *John Archer*	3.00
___ WINNING AT 21—An Expert's Guide *John Archer*	5.00
___ WINNING POKER SYSTEMS *Norman Zadeh*	3.00

HEALTH

___ BEE POLLEN *Lynda Lyngheim & Jack Scagnetti*	3.00
___ DR. LINDNER'S SPECIAL WEIGHT CONTROL METHOD *P. G. Lindner, M.D.*	2.00
___ HELP YOURSELF TO BETTER SIGHT *Margaret Darst Corbett*	3.00
___ HOW TO IMPROVE YOUR VISION *Dr. Robert A. Kraskin*	3.00
___ HOW YOU CAN STOP SMOKING PERMANENTLY *Ernest Caldwell*	3.00
___ MIND OVER PLATTER *Peter G. Lindner, M.D.*	3.00
___ NATURE'S WAY TO NUTRITION & VIBRANT HEALTH *Robert J. Scrutton*	3.00
___ NEW CARBOHYDRATE DIET COUNTER *Patti Lopez-Pereira*	1.50
___ QUICK & EASY EXERCISES FOR FACIAL BEAUTY *Judy Smith-deal*	2.00
___ QUICK & EASY EXERCISES FOR FIGURE BEAUTY *Judy Smith-deal*	2.00
___ REFLEXOLOGY *Dr. Maybelle Segal*	3.00
___ REFLEXOLOGY FOR GOOD HEALTH *Anna Kaye & Don C. Matchan*	3.00
___ YOU CAN LEARN TO RELAX *Dr. Samuel Gutwirth*	3.00
___ YOUR ALLERGY—What To Do About It *Allan Knight, M.D.*	3.00

HOBBIES

___ BEACHCOMBING FOR BEGINNERS *Norman Hickin*	2.00
___ BLACKSTONE'S MODERN CARD TRICKS *Harry Blackstone*	3.00
___ BLACKSTONE'S SECRETS OF MAGIC *Harry Blackstone*	3.00
___ COIN COLLECTING FOR BEGINNERS *Burton Hobson & Fred Reinfeld*	3.00
___ ENTERTAINING WITH ESP *Tony 'Doc' Shiels*	2.00
___ 400 FASCINATING MAGIC TRICKS YOU CAN DO *Howard Thurston*	4.00
___ HOW I TURN JUNK INTO FUN AND PROFIT *Sari*	3.00
___ HOW TO WRITE A HIT SONG & SELL IT *Tommy Boyce*	7.00
___ JUGGLING MADE EASY *Rudolf Dittrich*	2.00
___ MAGIC FOR ALL AGES *Walter Gibson*	4.00
___ MAGIC MADE EASY *Byron Wels*	2.00
___ STAMP COLLECTING FOR BEGINNERS *Burton Hobson*	3.00

HORSE PLAYERS' WINNING GUIDES

___ BETTING HORSES TO WIN *Les Conklin*	3.00
___ ELIMINATE THE LOSERS *Bob McKnight*	3.00

___ HOW TO PICK WINNING HORSES *Bob McKnight*	3.00
___ HOW TO WIN AT THE RACES *Sam (The Genius) Lewin*	5.00
___ HOW YOU CAN BEAT THE RACES *Jack Kavanagh*	5.00
___ MAKING MONEY AT THE RACES *David Barr*	3.00
___ PAYDAY AT THE RACES *Les Conklin*	3.00
___ SMART HANDICAPPING MADE EASY *William Bauman*	3.00
___ SUCCESS AT THE HARNESS RACES *Barry Meadow*	3.00
___ WINNING AT THE HARNESS RACES—An Expert's Guide *Nick Cammarano*	3.00

HUMOR

___ HOW TO BE A COMEDIAN FOR FUN & PROFIT *King & Laufer*	2.00
___ HOW TO FLATTEN YOUR TUSH *Coach Marge Reardon*	2.00
___ HOW TO MAKE LOVE TO YOURSELF *Ron Stevens & Joy Grdnic*	3.00
___ JOKE TELLER'S HANDBOOK *Bob Orben*	3.00
___ JOKES FOR ALL OCCASIONS *Al Schock*	3.00
___ 2000 NEW LAUGHS FOR SPEAKERS *Bob Orben*	4.00
___ 2,500 JOKES TO START 'EM LAUGHING *Bob Orben*	4.00

HYPNOTISM

___ ADVANCED TECHNIQUES OF HYPNOSIS *Melvin Powers*	2.00
___ BRAINWASHING AND THE CULTS *Paul A. Verdier, Ph.D.*	3.00
___ CHILDBIRTH WITH HYPNOSIS *William S. Kroger, M.D.*	5.00
___ HOW TO SOLVE Your Sex Problems with Self-Hypnosis *Frank S. Caprio, M.D.*	5.00
___ HOW TO STOP SMOKING THRU SELF-HYPNOSIS *Leslie M. LeCron*	3.00
___ HOW TO USE AUTO-SUGGESTION EFFECTIVELY *John Duckworth*	3.00
___ HOW YOU CAN BOWL BETTER USING SELF-HYPNOSIS *Jack Heise*	3.00
___ HOW YOU CAN PLAY BETTER GOLF USING SELF-HYPNOSIS *Jack Heise*	3.00
___ HYPNOSIS AND SELF-HYPNOSIS *Bernard Hollander, M.D.*	3.00
___ HYPNOTISM *(Originally published in 1893) Carl Sextus*	5.00
___ HYPNOTISM & PSYCHIC PHENOMENA *Simeon Edmunds*	4.00
___ HYPNOTISM MADE EASY *Dr. Ralph Winn*	3.00
___ HYPNOTISM MADE PRACTICAL *Louis Orton*	3.00
___ HYPNOTISM REVEALED *Melvin Powers*	2.00
___ HYPNOTISM TODAY *Leslie LeCron and Jean Bordeaux, Ph.D.*	5.00
___ MODERN HYPNOSIS *Lesley Kuhn & Salvatore Russo, Ph.D.*	5.00
___ NEW CONCEPTS OF HYPNOSIS *Bernard C. Gindes, M.D.*	5.00
___ NEW SELF-HYPNOSIS *Paul Adams*	4.00
___ POST-HYPNOTIC INSTRUCTIONS—Suggestions for Therapy *Arnold Furst*	3.00
___ PRACTICAL GUIDE TO SELF-HYPNOSIS *Melvin Powers*	3.00
___ PRACTICAL HYPNOTISM *Philip Magonet, M.D.*	3.00
___ SECRETS OF HYPNOTISM *S. J. Van Pelt, M.D.*	5.00
___ SELF-HYPNOSIS A Conditioned-Response Technique *Laurence Sparks*	5.00
___ SELF-HYPNOSIS Its Theory, Technique & Application *Melvin Powers*	3.00
___ THERAPY THROUGH HYPNOSIS *edited by Raphael H. Rhodes*	4.00

JUDAICA

___ MODERN ISRAEL *Lily Edelman*	2.00
___ SERVICE OF THE HEART *Evelyn Garfiel, Ph.D.*	4.00
___ STORY OF ISRAEL IN COINS *Jean & Maurice Gould*	2.00
___ STORY OF ISRAEL IN STAMPS *Maxim & Gabriel Shamir*	1.00
___ TONGUE OF THE PROPHETS *Robert St. John*	5.00

JUST FOR WOMEN

___ COSMOPOLITAN'S GUIDE TO MARVELOUS MEN Fwd. by *Helen Gurley Brown*	3.00
___ COSMOPOLITAN'S HANG-UP HANDBOOK Foreword by *Helen Gurley Brown*	4.00
___ COSMOPOLITAN'S LOVE BOOK—A Guide to Ecstasy in Bed	4.00
___ COSMOPOLITAN'S NEW ETIQUETTE GUIDE Fwd. by *Helen Gurley Brown*	4.00
___ I AM A COMPLEAT WOMAN *Doris Hagopian & Karen O'Connor Sweeney*	3.00
___ JUST FOR WOMEN—A Guide to the Female Body *Richard E. Sand, M.D.*	5.00
___ NEW APPROACHES TO SEX IN MARRIAGE *John E. Eichenlaub, M.D.*	3.00
___ SEXUALLY ADEQUATE FEMALE *Frank S. Caprio, M.D.*	3.00
___ SEXUALLY FULFILLED WOMAN *Dr. Rachel Copelan*	5.00
___ YOUR FIRST YEAR OF MARRIAGE *Dr. Tom McGinnis*	3.00

MARRIAGE, SEX & PARENTHOOD

___ ABILITY TO LOVE *Dr. Allan Fromme*	5.00
___ ENCYCLOPEDIA OF MODERN SEX & LOVE TECHNIQUES *Macandrew*	5.00
___ GUIDE TO SUCCESSFUL MARRIAGE *Drs. Albert Ellis & Robert Harper*	5.00

____ HOW TO RAISE AN EMOTIONALLY HEALTHY, HAPPY CHILD *A. Ellis*	4.00
____ SEX WITHOUT GUILT *Albert Ellis, Ph.D.*	5.00
____ SEXUALLY ADEQUATE MALE *Frank S. Caprio, M.D.*	3.00
____ SEXUALLY FULFILLED MAN *Dr. Rachel Copelan*	5.00

MELVIN POWERS' MAIL ORDER LIBRARY

____ HOW TO GET RICH IN MAIL ORDER *Melvin Powers*	10.00
____ HOW TO WRITE A GOOD ADVERTISEMENT *Victor O. Schwab*	15.00
____ MAIL ORDER MADE EASY *J. Frank Brumbaugh*	10.00
____ U.S. MAIL ORDER SHOPPER'S GUIDE *Susan Spitzer*	10.00

METAPHYSICS & OCCULT

____ BOOK OF TALISMANS, AMULETS & ZODIACAL GEMS *William Pavitt*	5.00
____ CONCENTRATION—A Guide to Mental Mastery *Mouni Sadhu*	4.00
____ CRITIQUES OF GOD *Edited by Peter Angeles*	7.00
____ EXTRA-TERRESTRIAL INTELLIGENCE—The First Encounter	6.00
____ FORTUNE TELLING WITH CARDS *P. Foli*	3.00
____ HANDWRITING ANALYSIS MADE EASY *John Marley*	4.00
____ HANDWRITING TELLS *Nadya Olyanova*	5.00
____ HOW TO INTERPRET DREAMS, OMENS & FORTUNE TELLING SIGNS *Gettings*	3.00
____ HOW TO UNDERSTAND YOUR DREAMS *Geoffrey A. Dudley*	3.00
____ ILLUSTRATED YOGA *William Zorn*	3.00
____ IN DAYS OF GREAT PEACE *Mouni Sadhu*	3.00
____ LSD—THE AGE OF MIND *Bernard Roseman*	2.00
____ MAGICIAN—His Training and Work *W. E. Butler*	3.00
____ MEDITATION *Mouni Sadhu*	5.00
____ MODERN NUMEROLOGY *Morris C. Goodman*	3.00
____ NUMEROLOGY—ITS FACTS AND SECRETS *Ariel Yvon Taylor*	3.00
____ NUMEROLOGY MADE EASY *W. Mykian*	3.00
____ PALMISTRY MADE EASY *Fred Gettings*	3.00
____ PALMISTRY MADE PRACTICAL *Elizabeth Daniels Squire*	4.00
____ PALMISTRY SECRETS REVEALED *Henry Frith*	3.00
____ PROPHECY IN OUR TIME *Martin Ebon*	2.50
____ PSYCHOLOGY OF HANDWRITING *Nadya Olyanova*	5.00
____ SUPERSTITION—Are You Superstitious? *Eric Maple*	2.00
____ TAROT *Mouni Sadhu*	6.00
____ TAROT OF THE BOHEMIANS *Papus*	5.00
____ WAYS TO SELF-REALIZATION *Mouni Sadhu*	3.00
____ WHAT YOUR HANDWRITING REVEALS *Albert E. Hughes*	3.00
____ WITCHCRAFT, MAGIC & OCCULTISM—A Fascinating History *W. B. Crow*	5.00
____ WITCHCRAFT—THE SIXTH SENSE *Justine Glass*	5.00
____ WORLD OF PSYCHIC RESEARCH *Hereward Carrington*	2.00

SELF-HELP & INSPIRATIONAL

____ DAILY POWER FOR JOYFUL LIVING *Dr. Donald Curtis*	5.00
____ DYNAMIC THINKING *Melvin Powers*	2.00
____ EXUBERANCE—Your Guide to Happiness & Fulfillment *Dr. Paul Kurtz*	3.00
____ GREATEST POWER IN THE UNIVERSE *U. S. Andersen*	5.00
____ GROW RICH WHILE YOU SLEEP *Ben Sweetland*	3.00
____ GROWTH THROUGH REASON *Albert Ellis, Ph.D.*	4.00
____ GUIDE TO DEVELOPING YOUR POTENTIAL *Herbert A. Otto, Ph.D.*	3.00
____ GUIDE TO LIVING IN BALANCE *Frank S. Caprio, M.D.*	2.00
____ GUIDE TO PERSONAL HAPPINESS *Albert Ellis, Ph.D. & Irving Becker, Ed. D.*	5.00
____ HELPING YOURSELF WITH APPLIED PSYCHOLOGY *R. Henderson*	2.00
____ HELPING YOURSELF WITH PSYCHIATRY *Frank S. Caprio, M.D.*	2.00
____ HOW TO ATTRACT GOOD LUCK *A. H. Z. Carr*	4.00
____ HOW TO CONTROL YOUR DESTINY *Norvell*	3.00
____ HOW TO DEVELOP A WINNING PERSONALITY *Martin Panzer*	5.00
____ HOW TO DEVELOP AN EXCEPTIONAL MEMORY *Young & Gibson*	4.00
____ HOW TO LIVE WITH A NEUROTIC *Albert Ellis, Ph. D.*	5.00
____ HOW TO OVERCOME YOUR FEARS *M. P. Leahy, M.D.*	3.00
____ HOW YOU CAN HAVE CONFIDENCE AND POWER *Les Giblin*	3.00
____ HUMAN PROBLEMS & HOW TO SOLVE THEM *Dr. Donald Curtis*	4.00
____ I CAN *Ben Sweetland*	5.00
____ I WILL *Ben Sweetland*	3.00
____ LEFT-HANDED PEOPLE *Michael Barsley*	4.00

Title	Price
___ MAGIC IN YOUR MIND *U. S. Andersen*	5.00
___ MAGIC OF THINKING BIG *Dr. David J. Schwartz*	3.00
___ MAGIC POWER OF YOUR MIND *Walter M. Germain*	5.00
___ MENTAL POWER THROUGH SLEEP SUGGESTION *Melvin Powers*	3.00
___ NEW GUIDE TO RATIONAL LIVING *Albert Ellis, Ph.D. & R. Harper, Ph.D.*	3.00
___ OUR TROUBLED SELVES *Dr. Allan Fromme*	3.00
___ PSYCHO-CYBERNETICS *Maxwell Maltz, M.D.*	3.00
___ SCIENCE OF MIND IN DAILY LIVING *Dr. Donald Curtis*	5.00
___ SECRET OF SECRETS *U. S. Andersen*	5.00
___ SECRET POWER OF THE PYRAMIDS *U. S. Andersen*	5.00
___ STUTTERING AND WHAT YOU CAN DO ABOUT IT *W. Johnson, Ph.D.*	2.50
___ SUCCESS-CYBERNETICS *U. S. Andersen*	5.00
___ 10 DAYS TO A GREAT NEW LIFE *William E. Edwards*	3.00
___ THINK AND GROW RICH *Napoleon Hill*	3.00
___ THINK YOUR WAY TO SUCCESS *Dr. Lew Losoncy*	5.00
___ THREE MAGIC WORDS *U. S. Andersen*	5.00
___ TREASURY OF COMFORT *edited by Rabbi Sidney Greenberg*	5.00
___ TREASURY OF THE ART OF LIVING *Sidney S. Greenberg*	5.00
___ YOU ARE NOT THE TARGET *Laura Huxley*	5.00
___ YOUR SUBCONSCIOUS POWER *Charles M. Simmons*	5.00
___ YOUR THOUGHTS CAN CHANGE YOUR LIFE *Dr. Donald Curtis*	5.00

SPORTS

Title	Price
___ BICYCLING FOR FUN AND GOOD HEALTH *Kenneth E. Luther*	2.00
___ BILLIARDS—Pocket • Carom • Three Cushion *Clive Cottingham, Jr.*	3.00
___ CAMPING-OUT 101 Ideas & Activities *Bruno Knobel*	2.00
___ COMPLETE GUIDE TO FISHING *Vlad Evanoff*	2.00
___ HOW TO IMPROVE YOUR RACQUETBALL *Lubarsky Kaufman & Scagnetti*	3.00
___ HOW TO WIN AT POCKET BILLIARDS *Edward D. Knuchell*	4.00
___ JOY OF WALKING *Jack Scagnetti*	3.00
___ LEARNING & TEACHING SOCCER SKILLS *Eric Worthington*	3.00
___ MOTORCYCLING FOR BEGINNERS *I. G. Edmonds*	3.00
___ RACQUETBALL FOR WOMEN *Toni Hudson, Jack Scagnetti & Vince Rondone*	3.00
___ RACQUETBALL MADE EASY *Steve Lubarsky, Rod Delson & Jack Scagnetti*	4.00
___ SECRET OF BOWLING STRIKES *Dawson Taylor*	3.00
___ SECRET OF PERFECT PUTTING *Horton Smith & Dawson Taylor*	3.00
___ SOCCER—The Game & How to Play It *Gary Rosenthal*	3.00
___ STARTING SOCCER *Edward F. Dolan, Jr.*	3.00
___ TABLE TENNIS MADE EASY *Johnny Leach*	2.00

TENNIS LOVERS' LIBRARY

Title	Price
___ BEGINNER'S BUIDE TO WINNING TENNIS *Helen Hull Jacobs*	2.00
___ HOW TO BEAT BETTER TENNIS PLAYERS *Loring Fiske*	4.00
___ HOW TO IMPROVE YOUR TENNIS—Style, Strategy & Analysis *C. Wilson*	2.00
___ INSIDE TENNIS—Techniques of Winning *Jim Leighton*	3.00
___ PLAY TENNIS WITH ROSEWALL *Ken Rosewall*	2.00
___ PSYCH YOURSELF TO BETTER TENNIS *Dr. Walter A. Luszki*	2.00
___ SUCCESSFUL TENNIS *Neale Fraser*	2.00
___ TENNIS FOR BEGINNERS, *Dr. H. A. Murray*	2.00
___ TENNIS MADE EASY *Joel Brecheen*	3.00
___ WEEKEND TENNIS—How to Have Fun & Win at the Same Time *Bill Talbert*	3.00
___ WINNING WITH PERCENTAGE TENNIS—Smart Strategy *Jack Lowe*	2.00

WILSHIRE PET LIBRARY

Title	Price
___ DOG OBEDIENCE TRAINING *Gust Kessopulos*	5.00
___ DOG TRAINING MADE EASY & FUN *John W. Kellogg*	4.00
___ HOW TO BRING UP YOUR PET DOG *Kurt Unkelbach*	2.00
___ HOW TO RAISE & TRAIN YOUR PUPPY *Jeff Griffen*	3.00
___ PIGEONS: HOW TO RAISE & TRAIN THEM *William H. Allen, Jr.*	2.00

The books listed above can be obtained from your book dealer or directly from Melvin Powers. When ordering, please remit 50¢ per book postage & handling. Send for our free illustrated catalog of self-improvement books.

Melvin Powers
12015 Sherman Road, No. Hollywood, California 91605